Praise for *The Ethics of Anarcho-Capitalism*

This is an excellent book on anarcho-capitalism. It covers all the bases, and then some. This is an enjoyable read, an easy read, and at the end of the road lies real insight. Five stars.

- Walter Block, author of *Defending the Undefendable*

I was dreading reading this, but it is conceptually excellent.

- Michael Malice, author of *The New Right*

This book uses praxeology to define libertarianism based on the non-aggression principle. Ancaps may find the implications disconcerting, or illuminating.

- Stephan Kinsella, author of *Against Intellectual Property*

For those who enjoy going deep into libertarian theory, the thought experiments and strategies in this book will prove valuable.

- Jakub Bozydar Wisniewski, author of *Libertarian Quandaries*

THE ETHICS OF ANARCHO-CAPITALISM

The Ethics of Anarcho-Capitalism

Kristopher A. Borer

The Ethics of Anarcho-Capitalism
Kristopher A. Borer

Keywords: anarcho-capitalism, libertarianism, ethics,
   freedom, capitalism, anarchism, praxeology

Version: 20200329
First published March 2, 2020

ISBNs
paperback: 978-1-951974-00-8
hardcover: 978-1-951974-02-2
mobi: 978-1-951974-01-5
audiobook: 978-1-951974-03-9

Library of Congress Control Number: 2019921009

Written using the Vim text editor (vim.org)
Book layout done with Scribus (scribus.net)

krisborer.com

to Jana

Contents

PREFACE

When I was 22 years old, I read that an individual's personality tends to solidify around age 25. Seeing this brief window of opportunity inspired me to be proactive about shaping my view of life. I wanted to decide what ethical and moral systems I would live by, so I spent my free time researching what was out there. I was shocked by what I found.

Shocked to find a simple, beautiful, and powerful ethical system. One that could catalyze rapid economic growth, technological progress, and crime reduction. One that could model the interactions of individuals and explain why some societies succeed while others fail. One that could help every person live life to its fullest. Its name was libertarianism.

I was equally shocked by how far the world was from the libertarian ideal. Terrible things were happening all around that I had never noticed. I needed to get the word out. So I mailed people books. I went door to door. And, of course, I argued on the Internet.

I was not able to convince everyone, or anyone really. But in going over the ideas again and again, I learned something important. There were occasional questions about how libertarianism works that I was not able to answer. I realized that my understanding was insufficient, and before I could advocate I needed to develop a better understanding.

Fortunately, libertarians have produced many excellent books, podcasts, and other media, which I consumed a great deal of over the last decade. My goal is to distill the most important things that I learned about libertarian ethics into one place, polish up some of the rough spots, and save budding libertarians a lot of time. Though this book does not have citations, I have tried to make it obvious which thinkers had the biggest impact on me.

Whether or not you decide to adopt the libertarian ethos, I hope that this book will at least make it clear what that is. And if you do decide to join us, then let me be the first to welcome you and thank you for your help. We have a lot to do.

Kris Borer
March 2, 2020

Jeffrey Tucker

"Freedom is the foundation for all wonderful things in life."

FREEDOM

Freedom is the ability to do what you want. So, it is just about the greatest thing ever. You probably already have some warm, fuzzy feelings about freedom—almost everyone does. Yet, hardly anyone really understands what freedom is. Fortunately, in the same way a physics class can provide you a deeper understanding of atoms and stars, this book will give you the basics of freedom.

But it gets better. When the idea of freedom crystallizes in your mind, you will discover that life is more interesting than you had ever imagined. You have billions of friends you never knew. You will start to see the hidden magic of human progress all around you. Best of all, you will get to glimpse an exciting future that is not only possible but already under construction.

It's not all sunshine and rainbows, though. The world is currently suffering from an acute lack of freedom. There are families that are sick and hungry. Some men and women live under the daily threat of government bombs, mafia guns, or a mugger's knife. Freedom is not just some academic idea that keeps philosophers up at night. It affects real people every day.

Soon you will know how all of the terrible and wonderful parts of life can be wrapped up into a single system of thought. You will be able to look at the world through the lens of freedom. From this perspective, you will have an unhampered view of some of life's most beautiful and most gruesome aspects. It may be jarring at first, but you will have a greater love of life when you see it more clearly.

That understanding begins by developing a rough idea of what freedom is. To do that, you will start by getting back to nature. Not in a fun-camping-trip kind of way, but in a stranded-on-a-desert-island kind of way.

Ayn Rand

"Capitalism has been called a system of greed—yet it is the system that raised the standard of living of its poorest citizens to heights no collectivist system has ever begun to equal, and no tribal gang can conceive of."

CAPITAL

Imagine that you wash up on the shore of a tropical island, naked and hungry. You are all alone. As you search for some food, your feet begin to hurt because big, sharp rocks litter the beach. You hate the rocks. This place is dangerous, and so you decide to name it Danger Island.

You make your way up the beach and force your way through the tree line and into the brush. You push through leafy branches and step gingerly over gnarled roots. It is slow going, but after ten minutes you notice that the ocean is out of sight. You worry about finding your way back until you realize you can still hear the sound of the waves rolling in and out.

Eventually, you find a coconut, but you cannot get the meat or water out of the shell. Two birds watch from a tree as you look the coconut over in frustration. Then you realize something. You make your way back to a particularly sharp rock that you had stepped on and sit next to it. Then you slam the coconut against it, timidly at first, and then more and more forcefully until it cracks. Then you feast. You head back into the woods and repeat the process a few times, but decide not to open the last few coconuts and save them for later instead.

Now with a full belly, you consider the rocks to be quite valuable. What changed? Nothing about the rocks has changed, but they have gone from seeming worse than useless to indispensable in an instant. All that shifted is how you perceive them.

It turns out that value is entirely subjective. If someone thinks something has value, then it does. On the other hand, if nobody wants something, all of its value goes away. People may disagree about how valuable something is, and one person may value something one day and disvalue it the next. Ultimately, these disagreements are actually good for freedom because people can trade things they value less for things they value more and everybody wins.

Subjective value may seem at odds with your experiences in modern society, where many things seem to have stable or intrinsic value. Rice is usually cheap, and gold is typically expensive. However, with any good or service people perceive it differently, and its value changes dramatically based solely on the person or situation. On your journey through Danger Island, and life in general, subjective value is a concept that will help you in many different ways.

Back to your island. You have some coconuts and a coconut opener. You don't have to worry about food anymore. So what do you do? If you are like most people, you start looking for other useful things. You find some sticks and leaves, and you build a little hut for sleeping and storage. Then you search out or construct other things that can improve your life. Eventually, you have enough stuff to be able to relax. Life is so much better than when you first got to the island, and it's all because of things that help you do what you want to do, such as clothing, shovels, food reserves, and so on.

This process of acquiring stuff to make life better is a big part of human existence. These things enable you to live the way you want, which, by definition, makes you freer. The general name for all these useful things is capital. Capital could be physical goods like a pile of coconuts or an ax, or it could be the knowledge of how to start a fire. Capital is just an abstract idea that covers "things that help you do what you want to do." People value these things because they can free us from the constraints of nature. Acquiring capital achieves a significant kind of freedom—the kind people spend most of their time pursuing.

Capital is anything and everything that people value. Since value is subjective, what is and is not capital is up to you and can change over time. When you became stranded on this island, you didn't have much capital. You had your body and knowledge. Being in a state of nature like this isn't much fun so, like you, most people quickly turn their efforts toward making very unnatural changes to the world: weaving baskets, molding candles, etc. You haven't made any candles yet, but you decide to start making a modest hat out of blades of grass.

Aside from the setting, there is nothing unusual about this. While you are stuck on the island, those back in modern society are doing the same thing. They are inventing new electronic gadgets, building houses, and so on. They have a head start but, given enough time, you could reinvent and build all of the capital that makes the modern world comfortable—right here on your own private island. Though that would take a long time on your own.

Fortunately, a few days later a famous actress named Annie also gets stranded on Danger Island. You show her how to get coconuts and open them on the rocks. She appreciates your help, and you two become fast friends. What is rewarding about having a friend, besides having someone to talk to, is that working together enables you to produce more food than both working separately. The additional output comes from specialization. If you are better at collecting coconuts and she is better at opening them, then you can each focus on what you are best at and get extra coconuts for free.

Think about it. If you can collect two coconuts per hour or open one per hour, then with 12 hours of daylight you could produce eight edible coconuts. If Annie can collect one coconut per hour or open two per hour, she can also make eight per day. Separately you can produce 16 in total but, if you work together, you can finish with 24. Each of you gets four extra coconuts every day just by cooperating. Alternatively, you could stop when you get to 16 and spend the spare time relaxing, making clothing to wear, or building a boat to get off the island. You and Annie discuss what to do with the extra free time, and she is emphatic: "Let's find a way to get home."

The advantages of specialization aren't limited to coconut production. If, for instance, one of you focuses on fishing and the other on making clothing, then concentrating on what you are best at still means you will be able to produce stuff more quickly. Your little society will accumulate capital faster than it otherwise would have. So, with two people you could rebuild modern society not just twice as quickly, but more than twice as soon as with one person.

This becomes clear as you assist Annie in building a hut of her own.

"Thanks for your help," Annie says. "I haven't worked this hard in forever. I thought I was in good shape, but I guess I was mostly trying to be skinny. Well, keeping the weight off will be easy now that my arch-nemesis won't be able to find me."

"Who's that?" you ask.

"Chocolate. I love it, and most anything made with it, too. Chocolate chip cookies, hot chocolate, you name it."

"I haven't seen any cacao trees around here, but if we find one we might be able to make some."

"I'm just happy to have anything to eat at all," she says.

You are too and, now that Annie is here, you will have more food than you would have had without her. Despite being accustomed to a leisurely lifestyle, Annie works hard and is soon getting stronger and more skilled. In a few weeks, she might be better than you.

Fortunately, you can still benefit from the advantages of cooperation even if, like some people, you are better than everyone at everything. Economists call this the "law of comparative advantage," which just means that, in your struggle for more freedom, other people are your greatest asset. Unfortunately, they can also be the most significant obstacle in your path.

Ron Paul

"Understanding the magnificent rewards of a free society makes us unbashful in its promotion, fully realizing that maximum wealth is created and the greatest chance for peace comes from a society respectful of individual liberty."

LIBERTY

A few weeks after Annie's arrival, an enormous man washes up on the island. You run over to help him, but he pushes you away.

"Are you okay? What's your name?" you ask.

"Big Billy," he says.

"Where are you from?" you ask. When he doesn't respond, you say, "You must be thirsty. Come with me."

He follows you back to camp, and you give him some food and water. As he stands looking around, you try to explain a few things.

"This is where I live," you say, holding an arm out toward your hut, "and over here, you can see Annie's place."

Big Billy just grunts.

Admittedly, it isn't much of a tour, but it is still fun to show off all of the things you have built so far. You show him a water container that you have been working on and a woven grass blanket that is in-progress, but he doesn't seem interested. You decide to skip to the main event and explain to him the coconut production process. You are excited to have another team member, especially someone so tall. You and Annie were able to specialize the work you were doing in order to be more efficient. This division of labor worked well with two people, so you can hardly wait to see what it can do with three.

Unfortunately, you soon find out that Big Billy does not want to help harvest coconuts. Instead, he decides to steal some of yours.

"Hey, those are mine!" you say.

Big Billy ignores you. When he finishes eating, he yawns and walks over to your hut. He tries to go in but is unable to fit, so he lays down under a nearby tree and goes to sleep. You see Annie walking toward you along the beach and run over to her.

"Someone just got here," you say.

"That's great!" she says.

"I'm not so sure," you say. "He might be disoriented, but I get the feeling he isn't very friendly."

Over the next few days, your fears come true as Big Billy continues to steal food and water. Instead of things getting easier with an additional person, life has become more difficult. You now have to spend more time collecting coconuts and less time building your boat. You are not able to do what you want to do, so your relationship with Big Billy is making you less free.

It turns out that there are only two kinds of interaction that people can have: cooperation or conflict. As you have experienced working with Annie, when individuals cooperate, they can make life better for all. Everyone can enjoy a little more freedom. On the other hand, Big Billy's behavior has made it all too apparent that when there is conflict, at least one person is less free. Conflict might make someone, like Big Billy, better off in the short run. He gets more freedom because he has coconuts to eat. But it always makes someone worse off as well. In the long term, conflict tends to make all individuals worse off than they would have been if they had found a way to get along.

Freedom can be limited by nature, or it can be limited by other people. When you want more freedom from the constraints of nature, the solution is capital. If nature makes the night too cold, build a fire. When you want more freedom from the constraints imposed on you by other people, what you want is liberty. Liberty is the absence of conflict. It is a type of freedom, and one that everyone could have today if people decided to stop committing crimes.

A world without crime is a good goal, but not an easy one. When people get together, it usually leads to more capital and less liberty.

Depending on where they live, they might have more or less of each. Some places are particularly bad and have low levels of capital and liberty. Nowhere is perfect, so for those who have a choice in where to live, that choice is often between a lifestyle with more capital and a lifestyle with more liberty. Because of subjective value, there is no correct choice, just as there is no correct choice if a Big Billy offers to let you pick which coconut he is going to steal.

Liberty is great because having it means you don't need to worry about thieves or murderers. There is no crime in your life. It does not necessarily mean that life is good—you had complete liberty when you first arrived on Danger Island, but your feet were bleeding, and you were dying of both hunger and thirst. That said, when you have liberty, you might be destitute, but at least nobody is making things worse, and nobody is preventing you from improving your situation.

Now, if a person only cared about liberty, they could get it by merely finding some isolated place to live where there is nobody to bother them. With nobody around, there would, by definition, be no conflict, though it might get a bit lonely. Still, that person would be giving up all of the additional freedom that comes from cooperation. It would be more fun to have both liberty and company. Is there a way to have the benefits of other people without the drawbacks? With some ingenuity and effort, it is possible to get very close to that ideal.

And if you can find a way for everyone to cooperate, you could not only make yourselves relatively comfortable while you are here but also get off the island as quickly as possible. There is just one problem: cooperation requires liberty. In other words, any time there is conflict, it is going to slow down the capital production you need to get home. That makes liberty something worth fighting for.

A few days later, you and Annie hold a secret meeting deep in the forest. In hushed tones, you come up with a plan to free yourselves from Big Billy's recurring robberies. The two of you spend a few hours searching and find a pair of hefty sticks. Then you use your coconut openers to sharpen them into deadly spears. You discuss whether to hide the spears or carry them openly, but Annie says it will be better to make your intentions clear. So the two of you head back to camp and stand tall, spears in hand.

The next time Big Billy comes to take coconuts from the two of you, you threaten him with violence. Well, Annie does, anyway.

"Hey!" Annie says, holding her spear in the air, "Stop stealing coconuts!"

You hold your spear up in solidarity. Big Billy looks back and forth at the two of you, laughs, and takes a coconut anyway. Without hesitation, Annie thrusts her spear and stabs him in the foot. Big Billy drops the coconut and then falls to the ground, clutching his foot. After he stops rolling around and screaming, he promises he will behave. Annie says he'd better, or he is going to be walking on one leg.

Julian Simon

"Adding more people causes problems. But people are also the means to solve these problems. The main fuel to speed the world's progress is our stock of knowledge; the brakes are our lack of imagination and unsound social regulations of these activities. The ultimate resource is people—especially skilled, spirited, and hopeful young people endowed with liberty—who will exert their wills and imaginations for their own benefits, and so inevitably they will benefit the rest of us as well."

COOPERATION

Now with three productive members of society, division of labor really starts to pay off. But things get a bit more complicated. Billy chooses to focus on fishing and being as far away from Annie as he can get. Annie mainly collects coconuts from different parts of the island. You decide to spend most of your time gathering edible roots and looking for driftwood. You can all get a balanced diet by trading. However, if Big Billy doesn't like roots, how can you get fish? The answer is simple: since everyone wants coconuts, you can give your roots to Annie for coconuts and then trade the coconuts to Big Billy for his fish. You all have more options for things to eat, which is a nice bit of freedom you got just by trading with others.

Economists refer to this as indirect exchange. One might think it becomes more and more difficult when there are hundreds or millions of individuals producing different things, but, instead, it gets easier. The reason is once a particular item like coconuts becomes popular for trading, everyone will start to trade for it, even those who do not want it themselves. People will accept it just because they know they can use it to get other things they want. Once something becomes a common medium of exchange like this, it is called money.

People have used shells, beaver pelts, cigarettes, silver, gold, and many other things as money throughout history. Regardless of the form, money is awesome. It is a type of capital that makes trade easier for everyone. The easier trade becomes, the easier it is for people to specialize in the work they do. This division of labor leads to a more rapid rate of capital accumulation, which means more freedom than would otherwise have been possible. But money makes you freer in other ways as well. Once everyone starts using money, prices begin to develop. When you have same-unit prices for everything, it is much, much easier to make decisions about what to do with your time and other capital. Should you spend a day fishing or diving for clams? The relative price of each will help you decide. Should you trade three roots for a fish? It depends on how many coconuts each root and each fish is worth. How long will it take to build a boat? It depends on the money you earn every day and the total cost of all the parts. Using money to help make decisions is helpful on a remote island, but it is downright essential back in modern society. Advanced economies produce a lot of freedom, but the job specialization and division of labor needed to build them require money. Complex economies cannot function without it.

So prices are a type of capital that is useful for planning. However, they do more than help you make personal life choices. They automatically communicate everyone's subjective values to everyone else, and they do so in a way everyone can understand. It's super complex in practice but not too complicated in theory.

You ask the others on Danger Island how many fish they would buy if the price were one coconut, two, three, etc. You find that everyone wants to buy more when the price is low and fewer when the price is high. Not too surprising. Next, you ask everyone how many fish they would sell at different prices. This time it is the reverse. People want to sell fewer at low prices and more at high prices. So at low prices, not many of you want to sell, and at high prices, not many of you want to buy. But in the middle, there are prices at which some people want to buy, and others want to sell. When people realize this, they trade. Over time, everyone will buy and sell until they are happy with what they have.

So now if you want to buy or sell fish, the price of the exchange will likely end up roughly where the previous trades happened. Anyone willing to buy higher already did, and anyone willing to sell lower already did as well. The price of trades has reached an equilibrium between the supply of fish and the demand for them. Things don't always work this smoothly, but you get the idea.

Because value is subjective, what someone considers cheap or expensive can shift all the time. People are free to change their minds about prices and quantities whenever they want, and they often do. For example, if Big Billy catches a large amount of fish one day, he would probably be willing to sell some of them at a lower price. His change in perspective could shift the price of fish lower, which reflects how abundant fish are in your little economy. The low price lets others know fish are plentiful, and it is a thrifty time to consume more of them. A fish does not have any objective value, but this process shows how money and trade convert everyone's subjective values into objective prices. Pretty amazing.

What is also remarkable is that prices occur naturally when people can freely trade goods and services. They are just one more benefit of voluntary exchange.

When you have many, many people, prices tend to become stabler and move slower. If ten people were fishing instead of just Big Billy, then when he had a big catch, the price of fish would change much less dramatically. What does this have to do with freedom? Well, just as prices themselves make it easier for everyone to do what they want to do, stable prices are even more useful.

Prices are also a way for everyone to help direct the use of resources. By deciding how much you think something is worth and then trading on the market, you are helping to run the economy. The combined efforts of everyone buying and selling leads to an incredibly efficient way for people to work together. It turns human society into a computer that can decide what to produce and what to consume in a distributed fashion. Nobody could orchestrate something so intricate on their own, but it can be done almost effortlessly by working together. Everyone contributes a little and gets back significant dividends in freedom.

This model for thinking about how the economy works is helpful even when life is much messier and more complex. Things will not necessarily have stable prices unless traded regularly. For example, you braided some twine out of plant fiber when you were making your hut. After Annie arrived on the island, you sold her some. Since then, the rest has been hanging on one of your walls. So you are surprised when Big Billy comes to you and asks you about buying some of it.

"How much for that thin rope?" he asks.

"What do you want it for?"

"What's it to you?"

You decide you don't care and offer what you think is a high price. It is much more than Annie paid, but Big Billy buys it from you anyway. The next day you see him wearing what looks like a bandanna. It is a roughly woven mesh of twine and leaves. The look is a little strange, but it seems functional, and somehow it suits him. And the hat will be much more useful to him than the twine was to you. You valued the coconuts more than the twine, or you would not have made the trade. Though the price he paid for twine probably won't be indicative of what he or Annie might pay tomorrow. You just don't have enough information to predict how twine fits into the island economy. If you started trading twine regularly, then over time the information from all of the trades would help you hone in on a more reliable price.

Now, all of this good stuff—prices, division of labor, etc.—only works if people are cooperating. Cooperation is when people interact and their actions are compatible. If someone causes conflict, the system starts to break down. In some parts of the world, two towns might stop trading if bandits take up residence along the road connecting them. Similar disruption can happen within a single city if someone inhibits the trade of certain types of goods or services. For example, back in modern society, governments will ban the sale of specific books, or to block access to certain information on the Internet. When people cannot trade goods and information freely, two bad things happen. First, individuals cannot get the stuff they want, so they are immediately less free. Second, it reduces the division of labor, necessarily slowing down the production of new capital. People are forced to spend more time doing things they are worse at, which reduces the amount of capital they will have.

That is why liberty is so significant. Without it, not only do people suffer directly, but the accumulation of capital can be reduced or even reversed. That hurts people in the short term, and it is destructive to freedom in the long run as well. Fortunately, you and Annie were able to protect your liberty today.

"How do you know how to handle a spear so well?" you ask Annie.

"Oh, I joined a martial arts gym when I was younger to add a few skills to my resume. I wanted to learn how to sword fight, but the sensei said I had to start with a bo staff. It's a simple weapon—just a long wooden pole. I ran out of money before I could start any other weapons, but I learned a thing or two about fighting with a big stick."

"Clearly. Did you ever use it in a show?"

"No, and it's not the most practical skill in normal life either. Can't exactly carry one around."

"Well, this isn't normal life. At least hopefully for not too much longer."

It seems to you that cooperation is better than conflict, and usually better than isolation as well. So why would someone want to engage in conflict rather than cooperate? One reason is that while conflict makes the world less free in general, individuals can still benefit from a life of crime. When Big Billy stole coconuts from you, his freedom increased. He got to eat without having to find food himself or work to produce something valuable to trade for food. It did not matter to him that you were sad and angry, or that you would be less productive because of it, or that it might prevent the three of you from ever building a boat to get off the island. For him, the short run was all that mattered. He preferred the immediate benefits to himself to both the cost to others now and any future costs he might have to bear.

The point is that the world is not so simple that you can flatly say that freedom is good, and therefore everyone should cooperate. Even if everyone agrees freedom is good, any particular individual can get more through either cooperation or conflict. Which method is better is subjective, but either choice will lead to predictable consequences.

Cooperation will produce more and more freedom for everyone. These general benefits can be proven theoretically, but also observed directly. Cooperation has been responsible for the vast improvements in quality of life around the world, both locally and globally. On small scales, neighbors create companies that achieve more than people working alone. Companies working together produce products that they could not have made on their own. Trade takes this to a global level, where food and technology circulate around the world. Millions have raised themselves out of poverty by working together with people they have never met. Even with your little projects on Danger Island, you have seen how productive cooperation can be.

Conflict, on the other hand, is win-lose. It can improve freedom for some but must always reduce it for others. Conflict has elevated a number of people to lavish lifestyles and lowered many more into misery. A burglar might make off with enough money to live easy for years, but the family he stole from might not be able to buy food for their children. Wars have rocketed military men to glory while sending millions to an early death. Naturally, conflict has led to some of the greatest tragedies in human history.

So, if you had no control over your role in society, but you were able to choose what society to live in, one full of cooperation would be the obvious choice. But this does not mean it is irrational for people to choose to be criminals. Criminals who manage to get away with their crimes can increase their freedom at the expense of others. History is replete with examples of scoundrels, like mafia boss Carlo Gambino, who chose a strategy of conflict and did very well for himself. Great for himself and other scoundrels, but bad for everyone else. Every conflict has negative consequences when it occurs, but also irreversibly reduces freedom in general. It is one of the greatest sources of human suffering and retards the progress of human society. Still, a life of crime can pay, and it is up to each person to decide which path they wish to walk, and what kind of person they want to be.

In your particular situation, it seems clear that cooperation is going to lead to the best outcome for you, both from the perspective of living comfortably on the island and potentially finding a way home. Working with the others will make you all more productive and give you the best shot at achieving your goals.

To maximize all the good things that individuals are doing and building and creating, you will have to not only refrain from criminal activity yourself but also help to keep the peace. You will need to protect not just your liberty but everyone else's as well.

At first glance, this doesn't seem too difficult. Just make sure everyone gets along and break up any fights that may occur. But conflict is not always preventable. Accidents happen. And when conflict does happen, it is not necessarily clear what to do about it.

Back in modern society, they have companies and professionals who specialize in this kind of work. It is a massive industry that needs to innovate continually to adapt to the ever-changing world. In the same way that there are companies that focus on producing clothing, they also have companies that focus on protecting people and resolving disputes. Private security companies will watch your neighborhood at night to try to prevent theft. If something does get stolen, private investigators will help track down the thief. After they catch him, there are arbitration companies for resolving what compensation is appropriate. Even if they never find the stolen goods, there are insurance companies that will help replace the taken items.

On Danger Island, you don't have enough people for all of these specializations let alone the knowledge or tools to replicate them. The three of you are all alone out here, so you will have to take care of yourselves. But where to begin?

The only place to start is with the basics. Liberty is the absence of conflict, but what exactly is conflict? Understanding that should help you avoid it, or at least resolve it when it occurs. Protecting liberty like this will allow everyone to benefit directly from more freedom. It will also allow your little society to have the optimal production of goods and other capital. That will improve freedom over time and, eventually, it may even be enough to get you back home.

Hans-Hermann Hoppe

"Alone on his island, Robinson Crusoe can do whatever he pleases. For him, the question concerning rules of orderly human conduct—social cooperation—simply does not arise. Naturally, this question can only arise once a second person, Friday, arrives on the island. Yet even then, the question remains largely irrelevant so long as no scarcity exists. Suppose the island is the Garden of Eden; all external goods are available in superabundance. They are "free goods," just as the air that we breathe is normally a "free" good. Whatever Crusoe does with these goods, his actions have repercussions neither with respect to his own future supply of such goods nor regarding the present or future supply of the same goods for Friday (and vice versa). Hence, it is impossible that there could ever be a conflict between Crusoe and Friday concerning the use of such goods. A conflict is only possible if goods are scarce. Only then will there arise the need to formulate rules that make orderly—conflict-free—social cooperation possible."

CONFLICT

You carry a few pieces of driftwood back to your hut and look around. You have picked the beaches clean all around here, so you decide that you will walk to the northern part of the island today to see what you can find. Driftwood would be useful, but a grove of coconut trees to harvest from would also be helpful. The best, though, would be more people. Well, assuming they want to work together. More people cooperating would mean more freedom. But you know all too well that cooperation is only one type of human interaction. New people might also prefer conflict.

Conflict has two harmful effects. First, it reduces freedom directly because at least one person is not able to do what they want. Second, it makes it harder to accumulate capital. Why save coconuts if someone is going to take them away? Having less capital diminishes freedom indirectly. So, for those that want to maximize freedom, it is essential to keep conflict to a minimum. That is what protecting liberty is all about. You have already spent some time thinking of ways to protect yourself and keep everyone living in harmony.

Most of the time, it is relatively easy. After Big Billy arrived, you built a simple fence around your hut to make it less likely that he would steal your stuff. You have also started to carry around an ax or a spear to discourage him from attacking you. Just as liberty makes it easier to accumulate capital, capital accumulation makes it easier to protect liberty.

Back in modern society, things like locks, video cameras, guns, and the Internet have all helped individuals protect themselves. It is not just physical capital that helps, but also social groups and organizations. There are security guards who protect people and their belongings every day. On Danger Island, there are not enough of you to have a security company, but Annie is handy with a spear, so you hire her to watch your things while you explore the northern side of the island. She takes the payment, sits down, and starts building a sandcastle. You watch her for a few minutes while she grabs wet sand and lets it drip out of her fingers. At first, it forms sharp peaks that look like stalagmites and, eventually, it creates craggy mountains. You don't blame her for wanting to do something entertaining. There isn't much to do on the island.

You head out and, aside from the hot sand, the walk is pleasant. You even manage to find some rainwater pooled in the shade. As you walk, the beach becomes soft and sandy, with fewer and fewer rocks. Then you begin to see small holes in the sand. Most are the size of an apricot, though some look large enough to fit a grapefruit. Each hole has a little pile of the sand outside which looks freshly dug.

Then you see one of the inhabitants. A crab looks at you from his hole and then seems to vanish the next instant. A second crab darts across the ground and dives into another tunnel. You wonder if these crabs are good to eat. If they are, then this trip may have already been worth it. A new source of food would improve your chances of survival.

The shore gets rocky again, but this time the stones are long and flat. If they were not so heavy, you might be able to carry them back and build a stronger shelter. Two or three stone walls would make storm winds much more tolerable.

As you get farther from camp, you notice something in the distance. It looks like a large mound on the shore. It looks man-made, so you step into the bushes and trees that line the beach to hide your approach. You creep in the shadows, carefully and quietly, like a sandy, sunburned ninja. From closer, the object appears to be a wooden cabin, and you start to wonder if you are hallucinating. When you finally get close enough to see it clearly, you suddenly recognize what it is: an old shipwreck. Most of the ship appears to have suffered damage from exposure, but the bow seems to be holding together. The part above the sand, at least. The buried portion could be in any condition.

In your excitement, you run over to the wreck and inspect it. You can barely read the ship's name on the hull: *Margit*. The stern looks like the ground engulfed it a long time ago, but much of the wood is still in good shape. If you could use this old ship to make a new boat, it would save you a lot of time and effort. But is it okay to take it for yourself? Someone owned the *Margit* at some point. Someone might even still be using it for shelter occasionally, though you don't see any signs of human occupation right now.

You glance around the area for other signs of people, but the only footprints on the sand are yours. You look around the woods a little, but nothing turns up. You hesitate, grip your spear, and then shout, "hello?" A bird circles above you, but nobody answers your call.

You make your way back to the *Margit* to take another look. Bleached by the sun and worn down by the wind and waves, the *Margit* would be debris. But you tug on the boards, and they feel sturdy enough. You run your fingers across the wood. Erosion has brought out the grain, and it almost feels like the wood has regrown its bark.

You take one last look around and then turn back. As you walk toward your camp, you wonder how you can avoid conflict in this situation. Protecting the liberty of three people is hard enough, but how do you avoid conflict with someone you've never met? To make matters worse, you're not even sure you know how to define what conflict is.

Sure, it is easy to think of examples of conflict: theft, murder, assault, battery, rape, slavery, and so on. However, a list of examples won't always be enough. To avoid conflict, you need a definition that you can apply to any situation, even ones that you have never seen before like finding half of a ship's hull on the beach of a desert island.

Given your list, you can see that conflict does not include all of the bad things that can happen in life. On your way back the wind blows some sand in your eyes, but you wouldn't say that is conflict. Conflict is something bad that happens between people. So that narrows it down a little.

Yet, not every bad human interaction is a conflict either. Despite all of the passion and shouting, when you and Annie spend an evening debating who the greatest historical figure is, that is not a conflict, no matter how vehemently the two of you disagree. Similarly, if Big Billy asks Annie what she thinks of him and Annie says she doesn't, then one or both of them might feel bad about it, but it is not the same category as theft and murder.

So even though you know that conflict is a type of human interaction, there are many other ways that people interact that are not conflict. How can you distinguish conflict from everything else? On the flip side, how can you recognize peaceful coexistence when you see it? Sometimes it is obvious. The first week after Annie arrived, the two of you worked together to build a wooden bucket to catch rainwater, and that was obvious cooperation. The first week after Big Billy arrived, he took the bucket without permission, dumped out your water reserve, and then used the bucket for firewood. That was an obvious conflict.

Unfortunately, it is not always clear whether an interaction is a conflict or not. For example, what if a mosquito lands on Big Billy's arm and you swat it with your hand, slapping Big Billy's arm to do so? You would have prevented the bug from biting him, but also hurt him in the process. The situation is ambiguous. Big Billy might be thankful that you saved him from the mosquito, in which case, there is no problem between the two of you. On the other hand, Big Billy might not care about mosquito bites and hate it when people hit him. In that case, there is a conflict. What is strange about this is that even though the two scenarios are the same physically, a subtle mental difference can change whether or not a conflict has occurred.

It seems that you could misinterpret almost any scenario you can imagine if you do not know what people are thinking. A young man breaking into a car might be stealing it, or it might be his car, and he locked his keys inside. A woman pointing a gun at a man might seem like assault at first glance, until she fires, he catches the bullet, and they both take a bow. A man traveling with a young girl could be a wholesome daddy-daughter adventure, or it could be sex trafficking. The physical behavior gives essential information about what is happening, but it does not necessarily tell the whole story. For that, you need something else.

When you get back to camp, you are still thinking about how physically identical scenarios can have different ethical implications. Annie's sandcastle is gone, but it is not clear if she, Big Billy, or a wave destroyed it. You see Annie munching on some dried seaweed while she washes fresh seaweed and spreads it out to dry in the sun. It has become an everyday activity, and you have started to recognize different varieties of seaweed. You walk over, and she hands you a piece to try. She calls this kind "green lasagna." The texture is strange on your tongue, and it tastes a little acidic, but free food is free food. Then you remember what you came to say and ask Annie what she thinks about the subtle ambiguity of physical situations.

"Have I ever told you about my big break?" she asks. You shake your head.

"Like many girls, I was naive. I thought that if I worked hard, stayed skinny, and kept auditioning, I would eventually make it big. Of course, auditioning doesn't pay very well, so I had to take a day job. A friend of mine got me a job driving shuttles at an expensive hotel. I'd drive important people to the airport, bars, etc. I had hoped it would be a good opportunity to network with big shots. One time I was driving a well-known cinematographer. I thought I was clever and left the radio on so I could sing along. You know, just casually show off my voice while he was in the back seat. After a song or two, do you know what he said?"

"What?"

"Turn that off." She laughs.

"If singing to your passengers didn't work, then how did you make your break?" you ask.

"Well, after a few months, I was getting pretty discouraged. No callbacks. No interesting connections. I started to wonder if I should do something else with my life. Then one evening I was out at a nightclub with some of my friends, and I got a call from the hotel's front desk. They wanted me to take the limousine and pick up some VIP from a much nicer club on the other side of town. I told them I was off duty, but they said that unless I wanted to be unemployed the next day, I would be there in 30 minutes. I didn't have time to go home and change, so I ran in my heels to the hotel parking lot and then drove like mad. I almost had an accident while I was trying to fix my makeup in the rear-view mirror and ended up just making it look trashy. But it was okay because I was only a few minutes late.

"Except, when I got there I couldn't find the guy. I ended up having to bribe the valet, who told me that my hotel guest was asleep at the bar. Nobody would go get him for me because they didn't want to get fired. I figured I was going to get fired anyway, so I left the keys in the ignition and went in to get him. The valet had the courtesy to at least help me skip the line, but when I got inside I was on my own and really nervous. The problem was that I started to notice famous people and got super self-conscious, especially given the situation with my clothing, hair, and makeup—I was a total mess.

"Fortunately, it turned out he was a total mess also. When I got to the bar I touched him on the shoulder and said I was going to take him home. He looked at me with this hazy glare like he couldn't decide if he recognized me or not. His shirt was half undone and stained with some purple liquid. I explained who I was and apologized for being late, but he ignored me and mumbled: "Alright, let's go". Then he almost fell off his bar stool. I could barely walk in pumps as it was and I had to more or less carry his heavy ass to the front door. Halfway to the door, he lurched over a trash can and vomited. I was asking myself how things could get any worse, and then they did.

"As soon as we got outside, we were swarmed by paparazzi. I could hardly see with all the flashing lights, but I managed to get us both into the back of the limo. I didn't want to go back outside, so I climbed through the privacy divider window to get into the driver seat, drove us back to the hotel, and had the bellhop take him up to his room."

"And?"

"And then I went home to get some sleep. The next day the photos came out and I got a call from the hotel saying that they were letting me go. I was so embarrassed. Have you ever felt like your life was over before it even got started? It was awful."

"So what did you do?"

"What could I do? I didn't want to talk to anyone, so I spent all day hiding in my tiny apartment crying, eating ice cream, and watching bad TV. That night I spent hours just trying to think of anything I could have done differently. I decided that I would go back to live with my parents and cried myself to sleep.

"The next day I woke up to my phone ringing. It was a call from someone explaining that I was being cast in one of the minor supporting roles that I had auditioned for. And they were giving me an advance. I couldn't believe it."

"Wow. All that just because everyone thought you went on a date with that guy?"

"Uh-huh. How's that for subtle physical ambiguity!"

As Annie's surprisingly appropriate story shows, physical evidence isn't enough to fully understand what is going on with a human interaction. Since mental states are an essential part of identifying conflicts, we know that conflict cannot be defined purely in physical terms. If Annie and Big Billy are wrestling on the ground, that could be a fight, or it could be a friendly jiu-jitsu match. How can you decide? You could ask them, but even if Big Billy says that they are just having fun, that is not the end of it. Big Billy might think it is just a game, but what if Annie believes he is attacking her? You need a way of taking into account not only what everyone is doing physically, but also what everyone is thinking.

Such an approach requires a definition of conflict that is abstract enough to apply to any situation, general enough to encompass everything that is conflict, but precise enough to exclude everything that is not conflict. This definition is critical because identifying a conflict is the most fundamental skill for protecting liberty. Naturally, if you cannot identify a conflict, you will not be able to resolve it when it occurs, let alone prevent it from happening in the first place.

Fortunately, a system for making such a precise definition already exists. It is called praxeology, and it is an excellent way of thinking about human behavior. So even though you don't know exactly what conflict is, there is a tool that will help you figure it out.

Harry Browne

"Every action committed by any human being has one common objective—to bring about happiness for the individual himself. That is the one thing we can say for certain about human action—it is aimed at happiness. Whether or not it succeeds is something else again."

Praxeology

As you lay in your hut and consider the relationship between a person's thoughts and behaviors, you realize that morning has come. It is time to get up. When you open your eyes, you can see the light sneaking through some holes in your roof where leaves have dried and pulled away from each other. You'll have to patch those later. For now, you stretch a little and consider how praxeology might help you define conflict.

Praxeology is the study of purposeful behavior. In other words, praxeology applies when a person does things for a reason, like when Annie rubs two sticks together to start a fire. Praxeology does not apply when a person does things reflexively or unconsciously, like when Big Billy sneezes or mutters to himself in his sleep. If you try to help Annie build a fire by adding wood chips but add too many and smother the flame, that is still purposeful behavior. The outcome was not what you intended, but what matters is that you had any intention at all. So the basic object of study in praxeology is purposeful behavior.

Purposeful behavior is a useful concept because, by definition, it connects the physical aspect of what a person is doing with their mental state. This connection always exists because when someone does something on purpose, they must have some goal in mind. They are thinking about what they want to accomplish and behave in a certain way to try to make it happen. This link between purpose and behavior is what will allow you to reason about things like conflict, where knowing just the physical details of a situation is not enough.

So now as a student of praxeology, when you ask, "What happened?" you are no longer interested in just knowing what someone did but also what their goal was. The intention behind the physical act will reveal the additional information you need to detect conflict.

When Big Billy picks up a coconut from your pile, is there a conflict? If Annie is watching, she would not necessarily know. From her perspective, he might be taking payment for some trade or service rendered. Or he might be stealing it. Asking Big Billy what he is doing could help, but it would not provide total certainty. He might lie about his intentions or yours. Even if he sincerely believes that he is allowed to take it, there could still be a conflict if you disagree.

In the same way, back in modern society, this might happen if someone sits in a seat that you reserved on a train. You might wonder if they sat there by accident, or if they are trying to take your seat. Your reaction will be very different depending on what is going on in their mind.

In your mind, at the moment, is the thought that it is time to get up and get something to eat. You roll over and crawl outside.

While you are coming out of your hut, you see Annie and Big Billy a short distance away on the beach. Then you see Big Billy throw something at Annie. You feel anger start to flare up, but then you remember that you should not jump to conclusions. It could be that the two of them are just joking around and having fun. Then again, it could be that they are both angry and fighting. Maybe it is more complicated. It could be that Big Billy thinks he is playing, but Annie believes he is attacking her. Or, it could be that Big Billy is trying to hurt Annie, but she thinks he is fooling around. You cannot know which of these situations is occurring just by observing what is happening physically. You need to understand what each of them is thinking to get a full praxeological picture. You start walking over to see what is going on but, before you get there, Big Billy runs off. Annie waves at you and then heads into the water for her morning swim. It seems like everything is okay, after all.

You decide to start your day with some fishing, so you grab a small net that you purchased from Annie and wade out to a sandbar. Annie is more of an active hunter and fishes with a spear, but you have found the combination of a net and some patience works better for you. As you wait for fish to swim by, you try to think about the earlier encounter from Annie's perspective. She was involved in the scuffle, and there was only one other person, so she was working with much more information. But not everything. She was fully aware of her own thoughts, but she would probably not know what Big Billy was thinking. So it would not necessarily have been easy for her to comprehend the situation fully, even though she was involved. She was able to observe Big Billy throw something at her, but she probably did not know what his goal was. Maybe you will ask her about it later.

Praxeology involves thinking about human behavior in a way that incorporates both what people do and their objective for doing it. When you consider a person's physical behavior and mental state as a single unit, it makes it much easier to reason about certain things, like ethics and economics. Economists call this combination "human action" or just "action" for short. You can discuss situations by referring to the actions involved, which are the combination of both the physical activity and intentions of each person. When Annie lays out on the beach to sunbathe, her goal is to enjoy the sun's rays. If you stand between her and the sun, you would cast a shadow and interfere with what she is doing. If she were laying on the beach only to rest, she might not care about a shadow, or might even prefer the shade. To know which situation you are in, you need to infer what is going on in her mind. Since Annie has many routines, it is often apparent what her intentions are without asking her. But deciphering the human action of others is not always so straightforward.

Just yesterday Annie took some dried coconut and tossed it into the woods. You never saw her do that before, so you wondered if it would be okay for you to go and help yourself to it. If she was disposing of it because she did not want it anymore, then that would be just fine.

If she was putting fruit in the woods to try to attract crabs or birds to hunt, then taking the fruit would interfere with what she is doing and lead to conflict. These are two different actions with the same physical behavior but different mental components. When you asked her about it, you learned that the fruit had rotted, and she was indeed hoping to use it as a lure. Only then did you understand her human action.

So what does this have to do with freedom and conflict? Well, when people cooperate, both the physical and mental parts of their actions are compatible. When two people dance, both their movements and their intentions are in alignment. When two people trade, the same is true. Cooperation is any interaction where each person's action is compatible.

This definition of cooperation has nothing to do with the specific content of human action. It does not care if you are walking or running. It does not care if you had good intentions or bad intentions. It merely states something about the relationship between the purposeful behavior of different people. If any set of human actions matches this definition, then it applies, regardless of what those actions actually are.

Reasoning about action in the abstract like this is what praxeology is. In a way, it is like algebra. With an algebraic equation like $y = 2x$, you know something about the relationship between two numbers without needing actual values for those numbers. Similarly, praxeology can be used to develop rules about human action without referring to specific situations.

When you return from fishing, Annie is already back from her swim. She trades you a coconut for one of the fish you caught. You know that this is cooperation because you both voluntarily gave up what you had in exchange for what the other person had. Whenever two people willingly exchange goods and services, you can observe the physical process of trading, but you can also infer the human action involved. You know something about what is going on in their heads because of their choice of behavior. You might not know everything about what motivated them to trade. Maybe Annie is craving fish, or maybe she just wanted an excuse to socialize. In either case, you know that her human action is compatible with yours.

In the previous case, it did not matter why the trade happened. It is enough to know that you each preferred what the other had, so you made a swap. However, sometimes it does matter, in a certain sense, why a person does what they do. For example, if Big Billy gives Annie a flower, you do not know why he is doing it. He may be trying to win her friendship, or it might be because he thinks the flower will poison her. If nothing alarming happens, then maybe his motivations are of little concern to you. On the other hand, if Annie gets sick from Big Billy's flower, it is critical to know whether or not he intended to hurt her. That is when the idea of human action becomes especially important. In a scenario like that, you would not necessarily care why he intended to hurt her, but knowing that was his goal will shape the ethical implications.

You see Annie working in the shade to open some coconuts and Big Billy walking over to her. After thinking about criminal motives and poison flowers, you are feeling a little paranoid, so you casually walk within earshot.

"Yo, Annie," Big Billy says as he walks up.

Annie doesn't respond.

"Do you believe in fate?" Big Billy asks.

Annie says, "No." without looking up at him.

"Well, I do. I think that we came to this island for a reason. That this is all part of some plan."

"So what's the plan?"

"No clue. All I know is it doesn't make sense for the three of us to all arrive on this crummy little island at the same time."

Annie doesn't respond.

"That doesn't seem strange to you?"

Annie shrugs. Big Billy stares for a moment. Then he throws his hands up in frustration and walks off.

You think that Big Billy does have a point, though. Being on an island with only a few other people feels a lot like being part of some laboratory experiment. On the other hand, a small setting is useful for some of the ethical concepts that you have been pondering. When there are many people involved in a situation, there can be an information overload that makes it difficult to untangle ethical problems. Having fewer people might help you focus on what matters most, like the actions of two or three people.

Anyway, now you have this abstract concept of human action. Human action is purposeful behavior. It is the what and the why of the things people do. Human action is something that every person experiences and can understand, both internally and regarding other people. You might not always know why a person does the things they do, but everyone can agree that much of human behavior fits the pattern of purposeful conduct. From this objective starting point, you can develop definitions that apply to human action in general rather than specific behaviors. Even better, because these definitions are rooted in a concept that is objective, everyone can agree on what they mean. To protect liberty, you want objective rules around and definitions of conflict.

You hang your remaining fish to dry and take stock of your current food supplies. It seems like you saved up enough to last for quite a while, so you feel comfortable working on a project. You come up with a few ideas and, after considering your options, you decided to spend a few days gathering rocks. When the collection is complete, you then begin to lay them out on a bare part of the island where they will be visible from the sky. After another day of moving rocks around, you look at your four giant letters: HELP. You haven't seen any planes fly by yet but, if one does, you hope they will see this message and care enough to do something about it.

Annie walks up and looks over your handiwork.

"This is a good idea, but you could have used a better font," she jokes. Big Billy comes over to see what you two are looking at and stares at the stones. After a few minutes, the three of you head back to camp. However, that night, Big Billy decides that he wants to send a different message. He sneaks over and re-arranges the stones until the letters read BILLY.

Even though you don't know that he has done this, there is now a state of conflict. Just as if someone were to poison you without your knowledge, conflict can happen even if the people involved are not aware of it. In this case, your intended action is to try to call for help by arranging the stones to say HELP. Big Billy is trying to arrange them for some other purpose. You can't both do what you want to do. In a sense, your freedom trades off directly with Big Billy's freedom. This tension is the common theme among all your examples of conflict: people try to do things that interfere with each other. They cannot all happen, so something must give.

On the other hand, when people do compatible things, then it is possible for everyone to get what they want. For example, the other day as you were working on shaping wood for the hull of your ship, Annie carved a mermaid onto the piece that you intended to become the prow. The resemblance to someone on the island was uncanny, so you laughed and carried on. Notice, though, that it was your interpretation of Annie's action that determined whether it was cooperative or not. If you had had your heart set on carving a shark on the prow, then Annie's actions might have led to a conflict. So whether what people are doing is cooperation or conflict depends on the perspectives of those who are involved. In one sense, it is subjective.

To protect liberty though, what you are looking for is an objective definition of conflict. That's why you need praxeology. The idea of human action itself contains the subjective quality of what a person thinks.

You are about to define one of the most important concepts in ethics, so it is useful to get technical for a moment. You have already said that human action is purposeful behavior. This idea applies to most of what people busy themselves with every day. It is both the what and the why of things that people do. With that in mind, you can define conflict precisely. Conflict is when people interact but their actions are not compatible. In other words, conflict happens whenever people engage in mutually exclusive human action. It might be the physical aspect of human action or the mental part that makes each person's action irreconcilable. Either way, the result is that people are not able to do what they want to do, which reduces freedom for at least one person.

Actions can be incompatible and cause conflict even when taking place at two different times. In the case of the stone letters, even though you and Big Billy did not directly interact, conflict was still the outcome. The reason is that your purpose was not just to arrange the rocks in a certain way, but to signal for help using the rocks. Your use of the rocks was an ongoing activity, though most of the work was upfront. That is why Big Billy's action created the conflict. If you had arranged the rocks for fun and did not care what happened to them afterward, then there would not have been a conflict when he rearranged them.

Conflict occurs when actions are incompatible. However, there is a lot wrapped up in that seemingly simple definition. It includes every kind of crime and excludes every peaceful behavior. You can describe every criminal activity by the actions involved and how they interfere with each other. For example, murder only happens when one person is trying to live, and another person kills them. That is why people are enraged at murder but only sad when they hear a story of someone who asks to be killed to end their suffering. Battery happens when one person hits someone, and the recipient does not want to be hit. Most people would be outraged if a stranger knocked them to the ground while they were walking on the street but would shrug it off during a game of lacrosse.

Describing conflict requires implicit or explicit acknowledgment of what two or more people are doing and thinking. It must also describe how the actions of those two people come together in an incompatible way. Whenever you encounter a situation where people are trying to engage in behaviors that will interfere with each other, you will know that there is conflict.

Conflict limits freedom, so it is vital to be able to predict, avoid, identify, and resolve conflict. If you can gather enough information, then you can use your definition of conflict to objectively decide when there is conflict and when there is not. That will get you one step closer to protecting liberty.

Your definition of conflict is very general, which might make it a little unintuitive. If two people try to stand in the same spot, then there is conflict. If two people try to eat the same plum, there is conflict. Sometimes conflict is obvious. Then again, sometimes it is not. You wonder if a soccer match should be considered conflict since both teams are trying to win but only one of them can. In reality, a sporting match is an elegant display of cooperation. Each player is trying to win, so their goals are mutually exclusive. Despite this, each person's action is entirely compatible with everyone else's. Their purpose is to play, and the game is only playable if both teams work together and play by the rules.

The same is true not just for sporting competitions, but also for competition in the economy. When two store owners compete for a customer, only one of them can win that person's business. But that doesn't mean that they can't both try. If one store owner offers certain goods and services, that does not prevent anybody else from providing other products or services, or even the same goods and services.

So long as nobody resorts to criminal behaviors, like physically attacking their competitors, then competition remains a type of indirect cooperation, not conflict. This is true whether you and Annie are trying to sell coconuts to Big Billy, or you and Big Billy are trying to buy fish from Annie. As long as everyone behaves ethically, then they remain in the realm of fair play called free-market competition.

A free market is a society without conflict. It may be competitive and the competition might be brutal at times. Competitors may even hate each other, and never consider cooperating directly with each other. But as long as they respect each other's liberty, they are acting within a broader framework of cooperation. Their goals may conflict, but their actions do not.

That is not to say that people never break the rules. The fact is individuals cheat in both sports and business. But if you injure an athlete's leg to take him out of the contest, you are no longer competing; you are a criminal. The same goes for a fisherman who sneaks over to his competitor's ship in the night to sink it. At that point, they have moved from competition to conflict.

It is often easier, and therefore tempting, to resort to conflict. Animals in the wild battle frequently, but, for humans, there is a better way. Competition is a productive form of cooperation that has allowed people to experiment with new ways of doing things. Better methods tended to survive and propelled humanity from savagery to a relatively peaceful and comfortable existence. If you can identify conflict, then you can help avoid it and keep society moving toward freedom.

Conflict is not always intentional, though. If you pay Big Billy to drag a log back to your hut, but he brings the wrong one, that could be conflict even if it was an accident on his part. The idea of manslaughter exists to distinguish accidentally killing someone from intentional murder. Both are crimes, but intentional ones are considered more severe. In either case, the criminal has some purpose, but for intentional crimes the purpose is to commit a crime, while for unintentional crimes the purpose is something peaceful.

So now you think you are starting to understand what conflict is. It is just incompatible human actions. Praxeology does not care about the content of action; it cares about action as such. So, this definition of conflict is abstract, which has the advantage that it is general enough to apply to any situation, even ones you have not seen before. It also has the disadvantage that it demands a lot of work to be used in practice. You need to figure out what is going on, what people are doing, and what they are thinking to identify conflict. If you have enough information and you understand all the human action involved in a particular scenario, then you can decide if a conflict has occurred or not.

You mull on that for a few hours. Later in the day, Annie comes back from a walk. She borrows your ax to open some clams that she found. Since she did not ask for your permission ahead of time, are you in a state of conflict? It depends on you, your opinion, and ultimately your human action. If you were saving the ax for yourself and had planned on using it to chop wood today, then Annie taking it would prevent you from doing what you want to do. Her action would diminish your freedom and result in a conflict. As it happens, you were not planning to use it today and are okay with Annie using it instead, so there is no conflict.

Unfortunately, things are not always this straightforward. Identifying conflict requires you to use your understanding of the world, people, and a given situation to get a handle on the human action involved. You might need to interview large numbers of people, consider long histories, and even sort out half-truths from outright lies. But, in the end, if you can use your experience and knowledge to learn what everyone's purposeful behavior is, you can figure out whether there is conflict or not.

However, once you identify a conflict, what should you do about it? In your quest for freedom in general and liberty in particular, there is still one missing piece of the puzzle. Once you identify conflict, what is the right way to resolve it? You think about this while searching the beach for new driftwood.

Walter Block

"The basic premise of [libertarianism] is that it is illegitimate to engage in aggression against nonaggressors. What is meant by aggression is not assertiveness, argumentativeness, competitiveness, adventurousness, quarrelsomeness, or antagonism. What is meant by aggression is the use of violence, such as that which takes place in murder, rape, robbery, or kidnapping. Libertarianism does not imply pacifism; it does not forbid the use of violence in defense or even in retaliation against violence. Libertarian philosophy condemns only the initiation of violence—the use of violence against a nonviolent person or his property."

THE NON-AGGRESSION PRINCIPLE

When you get back to camp, you find Annie and Big Billy fighting again in the surf. From their expressions, you can tell that they are trying to hurt each other. It's a real conflict. Unfortunately, just identifying a conflict is not all that productive. You need to do something about it.

You push them apart, tell them to calm down, and ask what is going on.

"She stole my coconut!" Big Billy says.

"Why did you take the coconut?" you ask Annie.

"It's my coconut!" she says.

You see the coconut in question sitting on the beach nearby. You recognize that you have stopped the fight, but you have not resolved the conflict. Unless you end the underlying problem, they will probably start fighting again, and everyone's freedom will continue to suffer. So how can you do that?

You can think of many different ways to try to prevent them from fighting over the coconut. You could split the coconut and give each of them half. You could try to decide which of them should get the coconut. You could try to wear them out until they give up on the coconut. You could try to take the coconut for yourself, though even if this stopped the two of them from fighting each other, it might cause other problems.

There are other approaches, too, and each has advantages and disadvantages. However, if your goal is to minimize conflict, you will have to find a solution that won't result in new conflicts. The best way is to find the source of the original conflict and put a stop to it. Once you know what happened and why, you will understand who is at fault. Then you can begin trying to set things right.

However, before you can determine the root of the problem, you first need to define what behavior is acceptable and what is not. For conflict resolution, you specifically need rules that govern how people should behave relative to one another. You can check what a person does against those rules to see if what they did is in accordance with them and then take corrective measures as necessary. These rules form what is called an ethical system. Ethics prescribes how to resolve conflict. Behaviors that follow the rules of an ethical system are considered to be ethical, while others are unethical. Ethics does not attempt to categorize action beyond this but instead leaves that to morality.

Morality defines whether an action is good or bad. Is it good or bad to always tell the truth? That is subjective, and the answer depends on your moral principles. Morals are an important complement to an ethical system. Morality covers not just interaction but everything a person might do. One important moral decision is whether to follow a particular ethical system, because it can have dramatic effects on your life and the lives of others.

For example, if everyone agreed to an ethical rule that says, "do not hit," then you would have to conclude that both Annie and Big Billy did something wrong. This rule is easy to apply but leads to some impractical results. An obvious one is that those who follow the rule are at the mercy of those who break it. It also has the negative side effect of prohibiting healthy, good behaviors along with bad ones. For example, a ban on hitting would prevent hockey, fencing, and even congratulating someone with a pat on their back.

The problem with banning a physical act is that every physical interaction might be conflict or it might not, depending on the preferences of those involved. Whether something is a social visit or trespassing, sex or rape, assisted suicide or murder, etc., depends on what people are thinking. You need your rule to incorporate both what people physically do and what they think. What you need is to use praxeology.

Since conflict is a type of interaction, someone must have done something to cause the conflict. In your quest for freedom, you are trying to minimize conflict. It follows then that you do not want people to cause conflict, either now or in the future. In other words, you can take the praxeological definition of conflict and state it as an ethical rule: Do not cause conflict. This definition gives you an abstract tool that can apply to any situation, even ones you have not seen before. It does not provide much guidance on how to determine who caused a conflict. However, as long as you can use your understanding of the world to figure that out, then you will be able to determine how to resolve it.

Annie and Big Billy are fighting. You establish that this is a real conflict. Now you need to know who caused the conflict.

"How did this all start?" you ask.

Billy responds immediately, "I saw her take that coconut from my stash."

"That's true, but I only took the coconut because it was originally one of mine. He stole it from me," Annie says.

"I did not," Big Billy says. "I found it on the ground."

"Where?" you ask.

"Near Annie's pile."

"How close?" you ask.

"About this far away," he says, holding his hands about a meter apart.

Annie butts in, "And it didn't occur to you that maybe it fell off my pile?"

"No. It was pretty far away," he says with a straight face.

After all that, you think you understand what happened. Now you need to make a judgment. Did Annie cause it when she took the coconut from Big Billy's pile? Or was it Big Billy's fault for taking the coconut from near Annie's stack? Are they both responsible to some extent?

If the coconut had been very far from Annie's pile, then Big Billy's excuse might have made sense. But with the gusty winds that sometimes come off the sea, it is quite common for things to get blown about—even coconuts. Conversely, if Annie had intentionally put the coconut some distance from her pile, then Big Billy's confusion might have been her fault. Given your understanding of the situation, you decide that Big Billy is the one who caused the conflict. Under the do-not-hit rule, Annie would have been behaving unethically. However, according to the cause-no-conflict rule, Annie's actions were entirely ethical when she took the coconut back. The same was true even when she used violence to try to keep Big Billy from taking it from her.

The cause-no-conflict rule is called the non-aggression principle or NAP. Aggression is any action that causes conflict. Such an action must be purposeful, but not necessarily intentional. You could cause conflict by intentionally or accidentally going into Annie's hut. On the other hand, it would not be aggression if you were asleep and a wave floated you from your own hut into hers.

To understand aggression, you must know the purpose behind what people are doing. Aggression is not a physical behavior but a praxeological concept. That is why even though Annie and Big Billy were both taking things and hitting each other, only one of them was violating the NAP. It's also why self-defense is often a valid excuse for doing something violent, like killing someone. Being involved in conflict is not against the NAP; only causing conflict is.

The non-aggression principle is an ethical rule against causing conflict. It therefore permits any action that does not cause conflict, even if the physical behavior would be a crime in other circumstances. Languages make distinctions between physically identical acts taking place under different contexts. Take, for example, the word pairs "kill and murder" and "sex and rape". Each pair describes physically indistinguishable acts. What distinguishes them is, rather, the context: "rape" and "murder" describe the initiation of conflict, while "kill" and "sex" do not (necessarily). Crime and aggression are the same thing according to the NAP. On Danger Island, you can rely on your newfound definition of aggression to decide whether someone has committed a crime.

For example, whenever Annie picks a coconut, she writes her first initial on it. Yesterday, Big Billy thought it would be funny to secretly write Annie's first initial on one of your coconuts. Then this morning, Annie saw that coconut, assumed it was hers, and took it. There is a conflict, but it is not theft. That is, the person responsible is Big Billy, not Annie. He is the one that caused the conflict by misleading Annie. In this way, you have identified a kind of crime: coconut ownership falsification. There is already a shorter name for this type of aggression: fraud. You can use the same approach to examine every kind of crime from first principles.

The process has two steps. First, you identify whether a conflict exists or not. If one does, then you know that a crime has been committed because a conflict can only exist if someone causes it. The conflict is not the crime, though. The actual crime is the action that caused the conflict in the first place. Whatever someone does to cause conflict is aggression and conflict is merely the effect of aggression. If you and Annie get into a fight over the coconut that Big Billy marked, that is not aggression. The aggression was Big Billy's marking of the coconut, because that was the ultimate cause of the conflict that resulted.

That is why identifying conflict is only the first step. The second step is to determine who caused the conflict. It may be one person or many people, but whoever is ultimately responsible for a conflict has behaved unethically. Knowing who violated the NAP and how, you will be in a position to start looking for solutions.

Praxeological definitions of ethical concepts like action, conflict, and the NAP give you an abstract framework for solving ethical problems. You then have to fill in the details to make use of them. The better you get at this process, the more quickly you can spot conflicts and their causes. This will help you prevent them, or stop them if they happen. In the long run, less conflict will lead to more liberty, capital, and freedom in general on Danger Island.

You pick up the coconut—the one Big Billy and Annie have been fighting over—and look at them both.

"Big Billy should have realized that a coconut next to Annie's pile was probably hers and not a wild coconut. So the conflict is his fault, and I'm giving the coconut back to Annie."

Big Billy clenches his fist. Annie picks up a rock off of the beach. There is a tense and quiet moment until a wave crashes to the shore.

"Fine," Big Billy says, leaving abruptly. Annie watches him go, then kicks the sand and sits down on the beach.

"I don't know what his problem is," she says.

"Raised by wolves, maybe," you joke, but it falls flat.

"It reminds me of growing up. When my siblings and I were little, we would all fight over food. It was never fair because my parents weren't around much, so the older kids always got what they wanted. Well, Mom and Dad, look at me now."

Annie stands up, and you toss her the coconut. She catches it and heads back to her hut. You watch her go and then turn to look out at the ocean. The surf rolls in and out, and you wonder how long you can keep Annie and Big Billy from killing each other. You decide to wait a day before trying to describe the non-aggression principle to them. That should give you time to think of a way to explain it clearly.

It is like a line drawn on the beach. Everything a person might choose to do is a grain of sand. On one side of the boundary are actions that will cause conflict, and on the other is everything ethical. In your quest for a peaceful society, it is necessary to be able to identify crime. However, it is equally important to be able to identify when an action is not aggression. You want to prevent people from violating the NAP, but not to go too far and prevent them from doing things that do not cause conflict. The reason is simple: preventing someone from doing something that is not aggression is itself aggression. If you had tried to prevent Annie from fighting to get her coconut back, you would have caused a new conflict.

Back in modern society, the line is not so clear. People are often able to do things that cause conflict without suffering any consequences. It is also quite common for people to restrict others from enjoying activities that are allowable according to the non-aggression principle. People decide that they don't like the way other people live their lives, so they threaten, beat, or kill them. For example, people throughout history have persecuted scientists for disseminating the results of their research. People sometimes even attack others, not for what they have done, but just for the way they look. As you ponder this, you hope things will turn out better here.

They can and will, so long as people abide by the non-aggression principle. It is a simple but powerful tool that you can use to analyze any human interaction, whether it has already happened or might happen in the future. Any time you want to know if something you did was ethical or not, you have to answer two questions. First: Was there a conflict? If not, then your action could not have violated the NAP. If there was a conflict, then the second question is: Did you cause the conflict? If you did not cause it, even if you were involved, then your action was still ethical. It is only when you cause conflict that you have done something unethical. The same approach can help you decide whether something you plan to do will cause conflict.

You take a moment to step back and consider where your thoughts have led you. You have an objective definition of conflict. Given enough information, anyone can apply your definition to people who are interacting and decide if there is a conflict. You also have an objective concept of causation. Every conflict must be caused by human action. With enough information, people can use their understanding of the world to determine the cause. But, these concepts merely describe the world as it is. They do not tell you how the world ought to be. The non-aggression principle, on the other hand, says how the world should be. That is subjective and categorically different from ideas like conflict and causality.

So, if you adopt the non-aggression principle, you are making a choice. You are stating that you value liberty and you believe that there is no excuse for causing conflict. This is not some universal truth; it is, instead, your subjective preference. You have crossed what philosophers call the is-ought gap.

The is-ought gap is the idea that you cannot derive what a person should do based solely on objective information about the world. You cannot prove that since Annie has experience acting, she should do a performance. Big Billy may think it is the best use of her time, but she might disagree. There is no objective way to decide who is right.

In order to decide what you should do about conflict, you need to choose an ethical system. You could choose among different ethical systems that already exist, develop a new one, or decide what feels right ad hoc. Whatever you decide, that choice must be informed by values outside of the ethical system. Maybe you think it has good consequences, or maybe you have other reasons for preferring it. The choice is yours, but subjective value means you can only make it for yourself.

For the same reason, you cannot merely tell others that they must protect liberty on principle. You can only appeal to their values. If they value freedom in general, or liberty in particular, then the non-aggression principle will be appealing. They will want to follow it and will wish others to follow it as well. Similarly, someone might not value freedom in the abstract but might genuinely care about things that liberty tends to produce. These benefits include more science, technology, and higher standards of living, including more food and education for everyone around the world. Others might care less about prosperity and more about peace, both among people who live in the same area and between those from very different places.

If someone values other things, then they might not choose to follow the NAP. A thief prefers easy money to honest work. However, even if someone does not personally want to abide by the non-aggression principle, they may still want others to follow it. A thief will have more to steal if the rest of society is wealthy, and the more closely a community follows the NAP, the more wealth it will tend to produce. The NAP maximizes cooperation, which makes the production of capital as efficient as possible. Even from the perspective of a criminal then, it is best if everyone else plays by the rules. He can enjoy more freedom if he is the only one who causes conflict and has a monopoly on aggression. For many, though, the NAP will be something appealing not just for others, but as the basis for their own ethical system.

The NAP is an ethical rule, and the ethical system built around it is called libertarianism. Philosophers would call this a deontological ethical system, which means it is a rule-based system rather than one based on judging consequences. The non-aggression principle exists to protect liberty, so the name seems appropriate, though a bit of a mouthful. If someone abides by the NAP, then they are a libertarian.

Libertarianism is not a complete framework for how to live life. It is just a simple ethical system that sets a bare-minimum standard on how people interact with one another. It tells you that there are certain actions you may not do, but does not tell you what you should or should not do beyond those. Should you be bold and try to escape Danger Island as soon as you have a raft that floats, or should you be prudent and wait until you have a more substantial boat? Should you be generous with Annie and Big Billy, giving them some of your food when they are running low, or should you be sparing and instead focus your resources on accumulating capital? These kinds of questions have nothing to do with conflict, so an ethical system cannot guide you. In situations like this, you will need to rely on your moral system.

For example, libertarianism generally allows you to use violence to defend yourself from someone who is attacking you, but it does not say that you have to. There is a moral system called pacifism that says you should not use violence even if it would be ethical to do so. So even if you decide to be a libertarian, you won't have a complete view of how to behave until you determine what moral systems to adopt.

If you have a moral system, you will know whether or not it is good to adopt the non-aggression principle. Libertarianism minimizes conflict and maximizes liberty, but is that the most important feature of an ethical system? That is for each person to decide.

Libertarianism also happens to be the ethical system that tends to produce the most freedom. This superlative may seem counterintuitive because libertarianism intentionally limits freedom. The non-aggression principle forbids individuals from doing things that they might want to do, which directly reduces their freedom. But there is no way to make an ethical system without limiting someone's freedom. Furthermore, there is no way to make an ethical system that applies to everyone equally without restricting everyone's freedom in some way. Libertarianism makes the best of a tough situation with a simple and universal rule, the NAP.

You can use the NAP to check things that you are planning to do or to resolve conflicts that have already happened. The more closely everyone can stay in line with the non-aggression principle, the more liberty everyone will enjoy. People are not perfect, though, so even if everyone were trying to be libertarian, there would still be conflict. Accidents cannot always be avoided. However, regardless of what happens, the NAP can be used to analyze any real-life scenario. You simply have to understand the human action involved, identify conflicts if they exist, and pinpoint the actions that caused the conflicts.

You have a lot to think about, so you decide to sleep on it. The night passes peacefully, and early the next day you head out to do some fishing.

There aren't many fish this morning, so you end up gazing around the horizon and staring at the island a lot. After a while, Annie gets up too. You see her head out into the ocean for her usual morning swim. Meanwhile, you see Big Billy walk down the beach and relieve himself in the ocean. Then he walks back, picks up his coconut opener rock, and tosses it into the sand. Afterward, he walks back to his hut, and you lose interest. Some seaweed floats by, and you collect it onto your shoulder for later. Not as good as fish, but better than nothing.

Annie finishes her swim and then stretches out on the beach. Some of her movements look like yoga poses. You decide to give up on fishing for now and start slowly wading back in to shore. Annie starts on her usual morning jog. Too late, you realize that she is heading straight toward the spot where Big Billy partially buried his rock in the sand. You yell to try to warn her, but as she turns her head to look at you, she steps on the rock and falls to the ground, clutching her foot. You rush over to see how bad it is.

"Are you okay?" you ask.

Annie uses some creative profanity to ask why someone would put a sharp rock on the sandy part of the beach. She has a cut on her foot that does not look too bad but is bleeding. Big Billy's coconut opener has some blood on it now which, you imagine, will make it less appealing for food preparation. Both Annie's run and Big Billy's breakfast plans have been impeded. There is a clear conflict here. Who caused the conflict? You know what happened physically, but now you need to try to learn what each person was thinking in order to understand the human action involved. Only then will you be able to determine who is responsible.

Perhaps Big Billy was only trying to get ready for breakfast. In that case, maybe Annie accidentally or intentionally caused the conflict. Possibly she knew or should have known that Big Billy's coconut opener was there, so it is her fault that he has to clean off his rock.

It could also be that Big Billy recognized Annie's morning routine and placed the coconut opener there in order to hurt her. It could have been a trap intended to injure her or exact revenge after yesterday's coconut incident. In that case, the conflict would be Big Billy's fault. Annie does not seem to care what Big Billy's intentions were at that moment, but she will probably be angrier if he had been trying to hurt her.

And what about you? You shouted at Annie just before she stepped on Big Billy's rock. That might have distracted her enough to change her pace. If you had not made a sound, she may have never stepped on the rock in the first place. You may be partly responsible for the conflict.

Because the situation depends on what people were thinking, there are infinite scenarios you could consider. To help narrow things down, you will have to gather information. If you can gather enough, then you will understand what people were doing and why, and you will be able to come to an ethical conclusion.

It seems to you that most of the work is not in applying the non-aggression principle, but in putting in the effort to fully understand the action involved. Once you know what happened, you think it would be relatively easy to decide who caused a conflict. Unfortunately, it can be challenging to discover what people's actions were holistically, mostly because of the difficulty of figuring out what they were thinking. This is doubly true after someone begins investigating a conflict, and everyone knows there will be consequences if they are found to be an aggressor.

Big Billy walks over with a stick and holds it out to Annie.

"Put this on the wound," he says. You can see some viscous liquid on the end of the stick.

"What is it?" you ask.

"It is pitch glue," he says. "It is made from sap and charcoal powder. You can use it to build things, but it is also good for protecting an open wound."

Annie takes the stick with only a hint of gratitude. She seems surprised that Big Billy knows how to make something so useful. You can think of more than a few ways to use a waterproof adhesive.

Big Billy's gesture and the way he spoke to Annie make it seem like he did not mean to hurt her. Though, he could be putting on an act. It is difficult to know what people are thinking, and you have to use whatever information is available to decide what their intentions are. The NAP tells you what to do, but you need to use your experience and judgment to carry the process out. In practice, that means you end up asking a lot of questions.

Unfortunately, when trying to keep the peace and protect liberty, you will not always have the luxury of enough time to ask questions. If a murder is going to happen, you need to act quickly. You will have to be able to look at any situation from a praxeological perspective and understand what is going on with the individuals involved using whatever time is available. That might mean making your best guess based on what you know and how the NAP might apply. All ethical decision making is time-constrained to some degree, but it is especially urgent when aggression is ongoing.

There is yet another problem concerning intentions. If you accidentally step on Annie's foot, that creates conflict. But after you explain that it was an accident, apologize, and make up for it, Annie can go back to living her life normally. If Big Billy intentionally steps on Annie's foot, that creates a conflict. But his behavior would also convey an implicit threat of further aggression in the future. Annie would have to worry about whether Big Billy will do it again, which creates additional conflict. Therefore, the NAP implies that intentional crimes are worse than accidental ones, other things being equal. This is in agreement with both intuition and existing legal systems. It is also another reason why it is so important to take a praxeological approach when solving a problem. Praxeology allows you to not only bridge the gap between the mental and physical realms when identifying conflict but also to determine the cause of conflict. If Annie threatens Big Billy the next time she thinks he is going to step on her foot, the intentional nature of his previous aggression could mean that he is responsible for the subsequent conflict as well.

Determining the relationship of actions over time requires a level of understanding that might take a lot of effort. You won't always need to start from first principles, though. The first time you encounter an ethical dilemma, you may need to use praxeological analysis and apply the NAP directly. If the same situation happens again, you will be able to reuse your work. After checking that the essential points are the same, you can reapply the previous analysis. If Big Billy does not learn from his past mistakes, he may end up taking another coconut from next to Annie's pile. The next time you will directly recognize what the resolution will be without having to do the heavy lifting with praxeology.

This reuse is essential because abiding by the non-aggression principle in everyday life would otherwise be a slow and painful process. Shortcuts can help resolve conflicts faster, make it easier to avoid conflict, and thus increase freedom in general. Luckily, there is already a well-tested way of doing this—getting most of the benefits of the NAP without doing lots of work all the time. You can supplement the NAP with a system that provides easy-to-follow guidelines that will help you avoid or resolve conflict in normal, everyday situations. People around the world already use it every day. This system is called private property.

Tom Woods

"One of the market's virtues, and the reason it enables so much peaceful interaction and cooperation among such a great variety of peoples, is that it demands of its participants only that they observe a relatively few basic principles, among them honesty, the sanctity of contracts, and respect for private property."

PROPERTY

The sun glides toward the ocean and makes the thin clouds in the sky glow like hot coals. Annie is down by the surf looking for shells and crabs that like to come out at dusk. You look at the dead tree you have been chopping with your dull stone ax and decide it is time to head back to camp. You collect wood chips from the ground to use as fire starters.

"You have won this round," you say to the log, "but I'll be back in the morning." The more time you spend here, the more you find yourself talking to inanimate objects. You wonder if that is a bad sign.

As the sun dips a toe into the water, Annie becomes just a silhouette against black and yellow waves. You watch her moving like a shadow on the wet, golden sand and see how she could be a star. Graceful and playful, she makes it seem like Danger Island is just a stage for some little production. You decide to sit on the ground and watch for a while.

Seeing her all alone on the beach reminds you of the first day you were stranded. You had picked your way along the rockiest stretch of the island's shoreline, looking for help. The coming of night had put an end to your search and made you wonder if you would ever see another person again. The days before Annie arrived were very lonely.

During those first few days, nothing you did could cause conflict because there was nobody else here. You picked a coconut, no conflict.

You put it next to your hut, no conflict. When Big Billy showed up and took your coconuts, it was obvious that there was a conflict and that he was responsible. Even now, with more sophisticated trading and production, because there are so few people, it is usually plain to see whether there is a conflict and from where it comes.

You watch Annie pick up a shell without causing conflict, and now you know that most of the things she would normally do with the shell will not cause conflict either. If she throws it back into the ocean, there will be no conflict. If she makes some jewelry out of it, same story. On the other hand, what if Big Billy comes along and breaks that particular shell? Would there be a conflict, and, if so, who would be responsible?

Surprisingly, whether there is a conflict in the last case is up to Annie. If she did not like the shell, then maybe there is no conflict. If she had plans for the shell, like making a necklace, then there is a conflict, and Big Billy is responsible, i.e., he caused the conflict. The only difference is Annie's thoughts. In essence, Annie gets to decide whether the way someone else uses the shell is ethical or not.

This situation of being in charge of an object that only one person can use at a time is very common. Whenever you pick a coconut, buy a fish, or build a hut, you have something that you are using for your own purposes. If someone else wants to use that stuff, then they have to be careful to use it in a way that is compatible with how you are already using it. Otherwise, they will cause conflict. If you are saving a coconut for yourself to eat, then Big Billy should not eat it. If you bring it to a beach party for anyone to eat, then he is in the clear.

In this way, the material things that you begin to use without causing conflict fall under your domain. They become a part of ethical human action, and others must take care not to create conflict by using them in the wrong way. The right way depends on what you are doing with them. However, your action includes your mental state and preferences, which can change at any time. Since it is hard for others to know what you are thinking, the safest thing for them to do when they want to use something is to ask you about it first. You can confirm whether or not what they want to do will be a problem. Just the other day, Annie asked if she could borrow your spear. Her spear had gotten stuck in a tree while she was hunting birds, and she needed yours to knock hers down.

You let her borrow your spear, and she returned it to you a few minutes later.

Every day, you use resources and then find yourself in this position of authority, where your discretion determines whether the use of some object is ethical or not. But the idea can be taken too far. If you go for a swim in the ocean, in a sense you are using the ocean. But that does not mean that other people cannot use different parts of it, or that you should get to decide how people use the whole ocean. The idea that your use of something prohibits other people from using it is only a function of the non-aggression principle. It applies to the uses or, more precisely, the actions, not the material things per se.

The non-aggression principle grants you authority because of scarcity. Scarcity makes it impossible for many things, like a walking stick, to be used by different people at the same time. The result is that when you are using something, there are very few ways that Annie can use it without causing conflict. Only one person can use your stone ax at a time. To avoid causing conflict, Annie has to ask you before she borrows it. Similarly, only two can sit on a short log before a third knocks somebody off. Waiting for one of them to finish first will keep things peaceful. Or, if the log is hollow, then the third person can crawl inside and use it for shelter without causing conflict.

When you find something in nature or are given something by another person, nobody else is using it. There are no other actions about which you need to worry. Therefore, the range of things you can do with it is relatively large. From your perspective, you can mostly do whatever you want with it.

On the other hand, once you start using it, the range of things that someone else can do with it is relatively narrow. Most of the things they would do with it will cause conflict because you are already using it. Moreover, it is hard for others to know precisely what options they have. Only you know what your intentions are, and you can change them, so you are in control. They can only use the object if you are okay with what they want to do with it. The judgment of the non-aggression principle, then, hangs on your preferences. You decide the fate of your things, at least from an ethical perspective. The facts do not always fit this pattern, but it is true often enough to serve as a general guideline.

For example, one of the first things you did after arriving on Danger Island was to weave a hat out of grass to keep the scorching sun at bay. Most of the things Big Billy might want to do with that hat would cause conflict. He can't wear it, or use it to start a fire or as a container to catch fish without interfering with what you are doing. The reason is that most of the time, you are using it for mutually exclusive purposes: wearing it yourself, collecting roots, etc. Even when it is hanging on the inside wall of your hut, it is part of your human action. You are still saving it for future needs and protecting it from the wear and tear that would occur if it were in active use. Just like keeping a coconut to eat later, it is continually part of your human action. If Big Billy tries to use your hat for something else, he will cause conflict. Then again, you could decide to use it in a way that is compatible with the way he wants to use it. For example, you could give it to him as a gift or lend it to him for a little while. In any case, whether Big Billy can ethically use the hat is up to you. The primary determining factor in this situation, and ones like it, is your mental state. So, an excellent approximation to the truth is to say that you get to control how people may use the hat.

This control happens so frequently that you already have some terminology that you can apply to it. Being in the position where your opinion largely determines how people may use a particular thing is called ownership, and the thing controlled is called property. Ownership is using a scarce resource in an ethical way. If you catch a wild fish, then you own it. If someone gives you a fish they own, then you now own that one, too. If you stop using it, then you have abandoned it and no longer own it. Ownership, in this sense, is a praxeological concept.

The converse of ownership is property. Property is any scarce means of ethical human action. It is whatever is being used, and by definition it is being used in an ethical way. Whenever you own something, you control it in an ethical sense. In other words, you mostly get to decide which uses of it are ethical and which are not. This right to decide is a handy convention and is purely a function of the non-aggression principle. Property is a useful concept for anyone who wants to follow the NAP but doesn't have enough information for a full praxeological analysis. Instead, they can focus on the physical resource under contention. Would it violate the NAP to eat an apple? First ask who owns it, and then ask them if they will allow it. There is no need to understand what they are doing with it. Instead, have them answer the more straightforward question of whether what they are doing is compatible with what you want to do.

Thinking in terms of material things has one advantage and one disadvantage compared to reasoning directly from the non-aggression principle. The advantage is that avoiding conflict is less mentally taxing. There may be many human actions, and each may be difficult to discern. Instead, you can focus on a single physical resource. Then when you need to resolve an ethical question, you only need to know who owns the thing in question and how they feel about how people are using it. This approach is usually much, much easier than trying to uncover the nuances of every person's behavior and mental state.

For example, if Big Billy goes inside Annie's hut, you do not need to go through the trouble of figuring out what he was doing and why. Instead, you can ask Annie if she wants him there or not. Easy. Ownership means you get to decide how people use something. If you happen to own something, then that means you get to determine what uses of it are ethical. Now the question becomes: How do you know who owns what?

People typically define the private property system with three rules that specify who owns each physical resource. The first rule is you own your own body. Second, you own anything that you are the first person to use. Lastly, you are the owner of anything that a previous owner gives to you.

So, you own your own body and can feed it, move it around, injure it, and so on. If someone else wants to feed it, move it around, or injure it, then they need your consent. Similarly, if you find a fallen tree branch that nobody is using, you could pick it up and use it as a walking stick, to build a spear, or as firewood. If someone else wants to use it for walking, stabbing, or burning, then they need your permission. Third, if someone gives you a stick and you decide to accept it, then you own it in the same sense as if you had been the first person to use it. These three rules tell you who owns any particular thing.

The first rule is called self-ownership, the second is called original appropriation, and the third is called voluntary exchange. With these rules, people can figure out who owns what, and then solve many ethical problems with minimal effort. There is no need for everyone to learn praxeology or explicitly understand the NAP. They can just remember who owns what, and then the owner can decide how to resolve any conflicts. If Big Billy owns a rope, he can swing it around all he likes. But if he wants to hit you with it, he needs your consent since you may not approve of the way he would be using your body.

With these simple rules, everyone can usually get along reasonably well. Instead of having to consider what everyone is doing and thinking every time you want to use something, you can ask what the owner thinks. As long as it is clear who owns what, then everyone can cooperate without too much effort. If you want to use Annie's coconut opener, simply ask her for permission.

You realize you have been using the idea of property implicitly ever since you got to the island. Most people back in modern society use it to some extent as well. It would be challenging for any society to function without some property system, be it libertarian or one that uses different conflict resolution rules.

Property and ownership are well-defined praxeological concepts, but the property system itself is not. The property system references the specific content of human action, which takes it out of the abstract realm of praxeology. This gives the property system the advantage of being a handy convention, but it does have a disadvantage. The disadvantage is that while the property system can be very efficient in many scenarios, it can also lead to incorrect conclusions in others. The reason is that it is merely a heuristic—an approximation of the non-aggression principle. The consequence of this is that the rules described above all have implicit exceptions. Even though they are called rules, in practice, they behave more like guidelines.

As you are watching Annie and thinking about property, you see a large, dark shape approaching along the beach. As it gets closer, you realize it is Big Billy. He has his long walking stick with him. Annie does not seem to notice him, and you start to wonder what he is after. He arrives behind her just as she is about to catch a shell rolling in the surf. When she bends over to grab it, Big Billy swings his stick and slaps her butt with it. She yelps, and he laughs. Big Billy winds up for another swing. You get up and start running over to put a stop to this, but as he tries to hit Annie a second time, she kicks the stick and breaks it into pieces.

Now disarmed, Big Billy retreats.

"Are you okay?" you ask Annie as you run up.

"Yeah, I'm fine." She picks up the pieces of the broken stick before the tide carries them away. You look at them and wonder who owns them now. Did Annie cause conflict in acquiring them?

"It's getting late," Annie says. "Let's head back."

As the two of you walk, you continue to think about what happened. Usually, it would be unethical for Annie to break Big Billy's stick. He owns it and should decide how people use it. However, if you look at the situation from the perspective of the NAP, you can see that Big Billy created a conflict, and Annie's response did not. As she did not cause a conflict, her actions were ethical. So even if you own something, you do not always control what uses of it are ethical. This caveat also applies to your own body. Others cannot punch you whenever they like. But if you try to steal something from someone, or attack them, then they have the option to hit you to defend themselves.

The exceptions to the rules have been areas where property rules have historically caused confusion. Self-ownership means owning your own body and has a strong intuitive appeal. From a property perspective, you do own your body and generally get to decide how people use it. However, there are cases where someone else might ethically be able to harm or even kill you. You remember when Annie stabbed Big Billy in the foot. When that happened, he was the one who caused the conflict. Annie was defending herself, so she was justified in hurting Big Billy. If Big Billy had never violated the NAP, then the idea of self-ownership would have been a reasonable way to think about the world. But once he caused conflict, it was more helpful to consider things from the perspective of the non-aggression principle.

Therefore, the property rules of self-ownership, original appropriation, and voluntary exchange are not absolute. This should not be taken to mean that there are times when it is permissible to commit aggression. Nor should it indicate that property rules are flexible and can be bent or broken when there is a good reason. The only reason to deviate from the property system would be to use a system that more closely approximates the NAP, or to apply the non-aggression principle directly. Whenever the ethical conclusion led to by property rules and the solution derived from the NAP contradict each other, the outcome of the non-aggression principle is the correct one.

The property rules can run into trouble in other ways, as well. Even if you never behave unethically, self-ownership is still not a strict enough rule on which to form the basis of an ethical system. If Big Billy pushes you into Annie, and Annie pushes you to the ground to protect herself, then you did nothing wrong, but neither did Annie. So self-ownership, just like ownership of any other kind of property, is only an approximation to the ethical truth.

The idea of original appropriation is another good approximation to the NAP, but it also has flaws. Usually, if Big Billy picks a wildflower, it will become his property. However, if Annie were about to grab the flower and Big Billy pushed her out of the way so that he could pick it first, that would change things. Even though he was the original appropriator of the flower, libertarianism would not say he is the owner. You would have to be the first user of something without causing conflict.

However, as with self-ownership, you can construct scenarios that form exceptions to the rule. You can come up with a situation in which the individual who originally appropriates something without causing conflict is still not the rightful owner. For example, if you and Annie are both competing to catch a crab, you might catch it before her and be the original appropriator. You may not have caused conflict, but if the only reason you got the crab is that Big Billy threw sand in Annie's eyes, you may not be the rightful owner from a libertarian perspective. These and other circumstances where the property rules fail require you to fall back on the non-aggression principle.

Even exchange is subject to being overruled by the non-aggression principle. If someone violates the non-aggression principle by trading or giving a gift, then the recipient would not necessarily become the owner of the item in question. For example, if Big Billy trades you a sea-shell for a coconut, normally that is fine. But if he had already taken money from Annie for the sea-shell, then that trade would be invalid.

The property rules defined above do not explicitly say what happens when someone wants to stop owning something. Implicitly, an owner can decide to stop owning something whenever they want. But how do you know when they have stopped? Physically, it may be indistinguishable from merely saving something for later. And how does this reconcile with the rule of original appropriation? The idea of being the first user could be problematic if taken literally. Falling back on the NAP helps clarify what is happening in cases of abandonment like this.

When Big Billy finishes eating a coconut, he always tosses the shell into the ocean. You, on the other hand, have been collecting your shells in neat piles around your hut in case they might be useful for your boat. Then there is Annie. Annie tosses her shells into the forest, but always roughly in the same place. She might be throwing them out like Big Billy, or she might be collecting them, out of sight. You know that if you gather the shells in the water, it will not be a problem because Big Billy had clearly thrown them away. But would Annie be angry if you scavenged for shells in the forest behind her hut? It depends on why she put them where she did.

In this case, it is easy enough to ask her whether she is saving the shells for something. However, this same principle applies to much more subtle and much more complicated scenarios. Is the shipwreck you found abandoned, or is someone still planning to return and dig the *Margit* out of the sand? How long are you willing to wait?

The problems associated with approximating the NAP are not unique to property rules. Another system, called voluntaryism, runs into the same trouble. Voluntaryism is the idea that voluntary interaction is ethical and nonvoluntary interaction is unethical. This turns out to be another useful but imperfect approximation of the non-aggression principle. It is simple to illustrate why voluntaryism is an imperfect ethical system using the following example: When a scammer gets someone to give up their life savings willingly, it is a voluntary interaction but not an ethical one.

Again, none of this should be taken to mean that the property system gives way when it is inconvenient. Nor does it mean that people should make use of aggression when they feel it is more practical or expedient. For libertarians, the opposite is true. Aggression is never acceptable, and any deviation from property rules should only be to more strictly apply the non-aggression principle.

Furthermore, the point of mentioning flaws in the property system is not to give the impression that libertarians should abandon it. On the contrary, even though the property system is not a consistent ethical system, it is still an incredibly valuable tool for freedom. All you need is to understand its limitations and act accordingly. The property system intentionally sacrifices precision for convenience, which turns out to be an efficient trade-off in everyday life. Big Billy does not want to discuss philosophy every day. He wants to know which coconuts he can eat. The property system makes it easy to answer questions like that and help people live in peace. Using the private property system can meaningfully increase freedom.

Despite its flaws, the property system works well, and a peaceful and prosperous society can be built using it. Moreover, it is a necessity for building large, complex societies. However, merely assigning ownership of physical objects is a little too crude for some of the more advanced features of a modern economy. You have even seen examples here on Danger Island where property rules were insufficient. Just because Annie swims in the ocean does not mean she owns the whole ocean. And recently, when your collection of driftwood got large enough, you needed a little extra storage space for drying out the wood. You paid Annie a one-time fee for space to store wood in her hut. Annie still owns the hut, but now you control some of the storage space some of the time.

The rudimentary property system outlined above does not provide a straightforward method of handling scenarios like this, where resources are jointly owned. It does not work smoothly with the ocean, where using it in one place does not always prevent others from using it elsewhere. Nor does it work well with land that many people use in common and over which no person has ethical control like they would over a single coconut. It also has trouble with scenarios like your storage agreement with Annie. People may want things that were previously controlled by a single person all the time to be jointly owned in different ways or at different times. As situations become more challenging, we can always resort to resolving conflicts with the NAP. But is there a happy medium where you can increase the usefulness of the property system to meet your needs without going all the way to praxeological analysis?

It turns out the answer is yes, and people worked out the details long ago. The property system can be made more sophisticated by moving closer to the pure action-based ethics of the non-aggression principle. The idea is that instead of all-or-nothing ownership of scarce, physical resources, you can have ownership of different uses of those resources. These uses are called property rights, and each property right essentially says that if you use a specific resource in a particular way, it will be ethical. Annie can sell you the right to store things in her hut without selling the whole hut. The owner of something gets a big bundle of property rights, related subsets of which can be sold off, rented, etc. The bundle of property rights includes every use of the item that is ethical and nothing else. So, while Big Billy owns his walking stick, he has the right to use it for hiking, but not for hitting Annie.

Thinking in terms of property rights allows for a closer approximation to the non-aggression principle while still maintaining most of the benefits of focusing on capital and owners, rather than actions. Property rights are a powerful tool in the pursuit of freedom. This improved approach enables people to develop a variety of valuable business relationships, financial instruments, and specialized rules for cooperation that power complex economies. Just as money helps people to trade and produce capital, the property rights system helps people to avoid conflict in an advanced, tightly integrated society.

Property rights work so well that people often mistakenly take them to be the basis for the libertarian ethical system. It is true that if you follow the private property system, you will get a mostly libertarian system. But that system will not be quite right—at least not all of the time. The property rules have exceptions, as you have seen, but these exceptions are tolerable because of how useful the property rules are. The exceptions are the price you pay in the trade-off for simplicity.

Is it possible to create property rules that do not have exceptions? Perhaps the ones you have been thinking about are too simple, and a better set of property rules would be just as good as the NAP itself. It is tempting to look for such rules because the idea of having or owning things—i.e., to possess property—is so intuitive and easy to apply.

Unfortunately, conflict is about intentional behavior, and only praxeological concepts can fully capture it. If you try to define a system for conflict resolution using any physical rules, you will end up with circular definitions. These definitions will always chase, but never quite capture, the human action involved. This is the fundamental problem with trying to base an ethical system on property rights. If you want a consistent system, you need praxeology and the NAP.

When you first defined the property system, the rule of self-ownership said that you own your own body. Later it became clear that this rule could lead to non-libertarian conclusions unless it is modified. Self-ownership says you own yourself but, according to libertarianism, this is only to the extent that you do not use your body to cause conflict. During a conflict, it may be ethical for others to exert control over your body. So, you cannot define the idea of self-ownership without the caveat that ethical uses of your body must be conflict-free. Because such a definition of self-ownership depends on the concept of conflict, conflict cannot be defined in terms of self-ownership without circular reasoning. So self-ownership cannot be used as the foundation of the libertarian ethical system.

Similarly, original appropriation says the first person to use something becomes the owner. You saw how that could lead to non-libertarian outcomes because someone could use aggression to become the first user of something. The rule, then, is often expanded to be: The first person to use something without causing conflict becomes the owner. Yet the goal is to create a system for resolving conflict. How can you resolve conflict using a system that requires you to already know who is causing conflict? The same line of reasoning applies to exchange. Again, the property system cannot stand on its own, without leading to circular definitions. It necessarily relies on a theory of conflict to be well defined.

This problem applies not just to the rules for assigning ownership but also to the idea of ownership itself. The property system says that you can use the things you own however you want, with the caveat that those uses must not cause conflict. But since all of these definitions rely on the concept of conflict, they cannot be used to define conflict or systems for resolving conflict.

This circular dependency is a real, practical problem for libertarianism. If you try to build an ethical system based on self-ownership, property, or original appropriation, it will run into issues. Your system will either permit some actions that are aggression, deny some that are not aggression, or both. If you try to save your system by conditioning it on aggression-free behavior, you will get closer to an ethical system free of contradictory rules. However, you won't get all the way there. You will have an approximation that works better but still suffers from edge cases and circular dependencies. For example, when a criminal causes conflict between two other people, the two victims may never violate the NAP themselves. Yet they could find themselves in a situation where they do not have ethical control over their body or property. This happened in the example where Big Billy pushed you into Annie, and Annie pushed you to the ground to protect herself.

These logical problems will allow critics to correctly point out examples where the libertarian-ish system leads to non-libertarian or incoherent conclusions. One such example is enough for critics to dismiss the whole idea of liberty and freedom, so it is critical to be as exacting as possible.

What is worse than leaving libertarianism open to theoretical attacks are the potential real-world consequences of implementing a flawed libertarian system. If you were to create a libertarian society based on an incorrect definition of libertarianism, that society would allow or even promote aggression to some extent. The laws, courts, and police would have to base their work on misleading premises, leading to more conflict than necessary and real harm to real people.

However, if you start with an independent, objective definition of conflict, then you can build a property system on top of it. Property is a natural extension of the libertarian conflict resolution rule. If you use it only as an extension, then you can fall back to praxeology and the NAP when property rules are insufficient. However, it is not possible to go the other way. You cannot take the property system and use it to build a libertarian theory of conflict.

So, while property is a powerful system for freedom and a necessary part of modern society, it is crucial to understand that it is only a rough tool for approximating the NAP. Property rights and the various business and legal systems that have been built up around them are similarly flawed. If one tries to treat them as fundamental, then the inevitable mistakes will lead to conflict and loss of liberty. If used properly, however, then these various systems will make avoiding conflict much, much easier. That means more freedom for everyone.

Now, property is such a wonderful invention that people sometimes try to use it in areas where it does not apply. A common mistake is to extend the idea of property to things over which conflict is not possible. For example, during your time on the island, you have come up with a good recipe for making fish stew. That procedure is knowledge, and knowledge is different from a physical resource like a shovel. Only one person can use a shovel at a time, but everyone can use the same recipe as much as they want without interfering with each other. So even if you are the first person to use a recipe, or someone gives it to you, that does not mean you can own it. You could try to keep it a secret, but if Annie comes up with the same recipe on her own, who are you to stop her from using it?

The real question is whether there is a conflict when different people use the same information or knowledge. Usually there isn't, even if that information is music, pictures, instructions for building things, or procedures for doing useful tasks. If you try to control the use of knowledge, you will prevent people from doing what they want to do. They will be less free, and you will end up causing conflict.

This type of aggression happens all the time back in modern society, where people try to stop others from copying data or disseminating information. These conflicts are another negative consequence of treating property as fundamental rather than instrumental. Instead, property should only be applied to scarce resources. When in doubt, rely on the NAP as a guide for unusual problems and only use the property system for routine situations where it can make things easier.

Making things easy is good for liberty. People can avoid causing conflict with less effort and, if conflict happens, it is easier to resolve. The less effort it takes to avoid conflict, the more time you have to do what you want. That means more freedom. It also makes it easier to acquire capital. When Annie arrived, you observed first-hand how cooperation can lead to much more rapid capital accumulation. With Big Billy, after a brief rough patch, specialization and trade grew even further. Now, the property system makes it that much easier to avoid conflict and keep interactions cooperative. More cooperation helps to develop the economy and, as the economy grows, people become wealthier.

In larger economies, markets, societies, and other systems become increasingly complex. Thus, property becomes even more essential, because there is more risk of conflict and more opportunities for cooperation. Yet it is important to remember that the ultimate arbiter of ethical behavior is always the NAP. Property is just a complementary system that makes following the NAP easy for most day-to-day situations.

Following a system of property, then, the three of you should be much more peaceful and productive. Understanding that the property system is just a tool and that the NAP is the true test for ethical behavior will help keep you from making mistakes. However, you worry that even with the NAP and the property system, you won't be able to protect liberty all the time. What can you do when, despite your best efforts, conflict happens?

Lysander Spooner

"All restraints upon man's natural liberty, not necessary for the simple maintenance of justice, are of the nature of slavery, and differ from each other only in degree."

JUSTICE

A week goes by with peaceful days and quiet nights. Gentle rains pass almost daily but, without enough wind to cause any damage, they only increase your precious water supply. One afternoon, you see that a water container has sprung a leak and hurry over to take a look. The water is draining rapidly, so you do the first thing that comes to mind. You lean a rock against the hole to plug it up. The stone stops the water from escaping, but you'll have to transfer the water to a different container to fully repair the leak with some pitch glue. Leaks like this are a problem but, fortunately, one that you can resolve fully with a little time and effort. Once repaired, the tank will function as it always did. After the next rain, your water supplies will be right back to where they would have been had no hole appeared in the first place.

In a perfect world, the consequences of conflict would also be reversible. In the real world, however, it is only possible to undo a portion of the damage done by aggression. When Big Billy stole Annie's coconut, you were able to make sure Annie got it back. But is that enough? Afterwards, she suffered the frustration and anger of being victimized. She also had to spend time and energy trying to retrieve the stolen coconut. Not only that, but she now has to worry about Big Billy taking coconuts in the future. You cannot undo many of the negative consequences of Big Billy's crime.

If you could rehabilitate Big Billy and show that he is no longer a danger, that would partially restore things to the way they would have been had he never stolen the coconut. Annie would no longer need to be afraid. She would, however, still have bad memories and would be lacking good memories from the experiences she was not able to enjoy. If it were also possible to swap the bad memories for the good, then that might set everything right. You cannot do these things, but they do serve as a useful point of reference.

You can compare the aftermath of a crime to the way the world would have been if there had been no aggression. You might call the latter the libertarian counterfactual. It is the life that a victim would have enjoyed if not for the conflict. Getting the real world as close to that reference is justice's goal. That is, not only stopping crimes but also moving the world closer to what its state would have been had no crime been committed. Justice is undoing the consequences of aggression.

But without technology indistinguishable from magic, you won't be able to turn back time and set things right. Still, are there other things you can do that will move the world in the right direction?

Back in modern society, if someone steals money from you, then you might spend a year chasing them to get it back. In that case, the libertarian counterfactual is not that you would have held your money for a year as, more likely, you would have put it into a bank account and earned interest. Instead of just taking your money back then, it would be more restitutive to take some additional money as well. Not to mention that instead of hunting down the criminal, you might have been working and earning money, so perhaps it would be ethical to take even more money than that. There are many hypothetical outcomes to explore, but the general idea is that justice might sometimes allow a victim to take more compensation from a criminal than what is obvious. Restitution is any action that brings about justice. Restitution could be returning stolen property, compensating a victim for losses, or any other action that brings justice.

Justice and restitution are praxeological concepts, so their application to real scenarios is highly situational. A criminal's actions lead to a conflict, within which you might use violence to defend yourself, your property, and even take some of their property. It is not usually aggression if you punch a mugger or tackle a thief before he can escape with your money. Similarly, it will not always cause conflict to take more from the thief than was initially stolen, or even to physically beat an attacker a little more than necessary to stop the crime.

The option to go beyond the obvious does not mean that victims have carte blanche to do whatever they want to criminals. The NAP only allows you to restore what was lost, not to take arbitrary measures to benefit the victim at the expense of the criminal. The point is that what is lost is not just the stolen property. The victim also misses the opportunity for self-determination—to live that part of their life with liberty. That opportunity is gone forever. The goal is to achieve as much restitution as possible without committing any aggression.

The idea that the NAP prohibits excessively large reactions to criminal behavior is known as the principle of proportionality. If Big Billy steals a coconut from you but then returns it out of guilt a short while later, then maybe one additional coconut would be the right restitution. If, instead, you were to take everything he owns from him, that would not get you back to the libertarian counterfactual, but move you to an entirely different situation. It would end up being theft in disguise, and you would actually cause conflict by taking an inappropriate amount of wealth in the name of restitution.

From the perspective of justice, it does not matter if aggression has already happened or is in progress. The goal is the same: to get back to the way things would have been if no conflict had ever occurred. Thus, the principle of proportionality applies to self-defense as well. When Annie speared Big Billy in the foot to stop him from stealing, that seemed about right to you given the circumstances. Much less, and Big Billy probably would not have stopped. And since the foot injury was enough to end the immediate aggression and make Big Billy promise to stop stealing, much more would have been unnecessary. If the conflict had been less severe, and her response had been more drastic, things might be different. If Big Billy stepped on her foot, and her response was to kill him, that would go beyond restitution. The disproportionate response would likely be aggression.

Note that justice is not only concerned with the immediate actions involved in aggression but also whether a criminal might decide to commit crimes in the future. If Annie had only whacked Big Billy on the hand, that might have stopped him from stealing that day but not convinced him to stop altogether. You and Annie would then have to worry about Big Billy every day, taking you further away from the libertarian counterfactual. In that case, it was ethical to injure Big Billy more than enough to stop the immediate threat—enough to prevent its return as well.

However, Annie was not ethically obligated to fight back. The NAP does not require a libertarian to pursue justice. It is consistent with libertarianism to be a pacifist and let criminals do whatever they wish. And in some cases, this may be the best strategy for an individual or group of people. Except in the rare case when only one action is ethically permissible, libertarianism does not tell you what to do.

Therefore, either a whack or a stab—or simply ignoring Big Billy and letting him steal her coconut—were ethical choices, and Annie was well within her rights to choose whichever course of action. But if her goal was justice, then the stab was the best option. The appropriateness of any action toward justice must look beyond the immediate effects of aggression. It must consider all the ways in which the world has diverged from what it should have been like.

This comprehensive view is also why you would generally be less upset by an accidental conflict than an intentional one. If you and Annie bump into each other while swimming in the ocean, it may be uncomfortable for a moment, but that is the end of it. You can go your separate ways and forget it ever happened. On the other hand, if she had bumped into you on purpose, then you would have to worry about her coming after you each time you are in the water. In the second case, you get the physical suffering, but you also have the stress of worrying about future conflicts. Though both situations are physically similar, the magnitude of the conflict can differ purely because of the thoughts of those involved. The mental aspect affects not just your understanding of the conflict, but also what restitution would be just.

Restitution and justice are praxeological concepts like the non-aggression principle. Indeed, the fundamental idea on which to base them is the NAP. You cannot understand what justice would be without being able to compare reality with what would have occurred had nobody violated the NAP. You cannot define restitution without understanding justice and keeping the NAP in mind to ensure that any action aimed at restitution does not cause conflict.

It is tempting to try to devise a general physical rule for restitution. An eye for an eye. Or, in the case of theft, maybe the stolen amount plus interest and the cost of recovery. However, this would be to make the same mistake as trying to create physical rules for resolving conflicts. At its core, justice is about human action, so only praxeological definitions can ever correctly model it. Strict rules based on quantitative measures will necessarily under- or overcompensate victims. Undercompensation will never reach the libertarian counterfactual. Overcompensation will cause conflict, and move away from it.

That said, it is perfectly reasonable to set up guidelines for restitution that are physical in nature. Just as ethical analysis saw big efficiency gains by using the property system, courts can develop guidelines for how to handle restitution in specific situations. These won't be universal rules that apply everywhere but, within particular societies and contexts, they can be beneficial.

You sit down to start patching the broken water container. While you are working, Annie walks up to watch.

"Everything okay?" she asks.

"I'm worried that I have been going too easy on Big Billy," you say. "When he steals things, I've only been focusing on returning the stolen goods, but not the lost time, effort, and agony due to the conflict. If I don't take those into account, the restitution won't be correct."

She thinks for a moment and then says, "My voice instructor always insisted on perfection. Not just singing the right notes but appropriate timbre and emotion. The right posture and facial expressions. Over four years, she only ever gave me a single compliment. It was just after I finished a song and she said, 'now that is something people would pay to hear.' It was frustrating at the time, but I think it's good to push yourself and strive for perfection, even if you never get there.

"That said, we're on a damned island in the middle of who-knows-what ocean. If I get my stuff back, that's good enough for now. If we ever make it off of here, sooner or later Big Billy will get what he deserves."

You consider that and realize libertarianism does not have an independent notion of punishment. When there is a conflict, the only goal is to make things right for the victim. Any negative consequences for the criminal are merely necessary components of restitution. The NAP does not say to punish criminals or to do anything harmful to them at all. The NAP merely permits libertarians to take whatever actions will not cause conflict. If you choose to pursue justice, then your acts of restitution will be only those actions required for the benefit of the victim. If restitution harms a criminal, it is only a side effect.

On the other hand, restitution might appear to be punishment, especially if it aims to prevent further crimes. If a criminal is likely to continue engaging in aggression, the only way for the victim to be safe might be to punish the criminal, so that they decide to change their ways. If rehabilitation fails, you may need to imprison the criminal. If imprisonment is not possible, then the criminal might even need to be killed. That is bad for the criminal, but the point is not to inflict pain and suffering on the criminal. These actions are only taken to try to restore the libertarian counterfactual. Since punishment is not mandatory in a libertarian society, victims can choose to be pacifists. They can decide that a criminal should suffer no negative consequences whatsoever. Pacifism may or may not be a good strategy for freedom, but it is at least consistent with the NAP.

The praxeological nature of restitution is why a wealthy person in a libertarian society cannot commit crimes with impunity by merely paying off victims. The appropriate restitution should be at a level that deters future aggression, which may be dependent on how wealthy a person is. If you try to set a fixed amount of restitution for a given crime, then the wealthy might be incentivized to commit crimes because they can afford it. The poor might also be incentivized to commit crimes if the penalty for a first crime is so high that there is no apparent marginal cost to additional crimes.

It may not always be clear how exactly to compensate someone for lost time, pain, and suffering during the crime, as well as anxiety and worry afterward, etc. When someone steals money or other physical goods, there are clearly defined objects to return to the victim. There are ways of quantifying the costs of resolving the conflict. But there is no obvious way of quantifying the subjective experiences of a victim or comparing them to what they would have been had the crime never occurred.

Justice is more challenging when a victim dies. In that case, restitution might include compensating their heirs. But restitution is still possible even if no heirs are available. A murderer cannot bring their victim back to life, but they can still do other things to try to move the world toward the libertarian counterfactual. The criminal would need to figure out what the victim would have wanted. Perhaps they would have wanted the criminal to dedicate their life to an important cause or to join them in oblivion.

When trying to decide what kind of recompense is just, you will need to use your understanding of the situation and the people involved. If Big Billy goes into Annie's hut without her permission, the level of restitution would depend on how she feels about it. If it terrifies Annie, then you would consider greater restitution than if you knew that it only bothered her a little bit.

"Speaking of criminals getting their due," Annie says, "what do you think about stealing from criminals? Like, if Big Billy steals a coconut from you, does that mean I can take it from him? It's not really his, after all."

"Would you be giving the coconut back to me?"

"I don't know. Do I have to?"

You take a few moments to think of different scenarios. When Big Billy takes your coconut, there is a conflict, and it is his fault. If Annie then takes the coconut from him, there is another conflict. If she is taking the coconut to give it back to you, then the second conflict is only between her and Big Billy. Big Billy is responsible for the second conflict because of his stealing in the first place, so Annie is doing something ethical and also bringing about some justice.

If Annie takes the coconut intending to deprive Big Billy of the stolen property, then there would be no conflict between you and her. You both want to deny Big Billy the property. The question is: What happens next?

If Annie takes the coconut intending to keep it, then there might be a conflict between you and her. If so, Annie caused a conflict in this case. The same might be true if Big Billy had a change of heart and was going to return the coconut, but Annie prevented him from doing so.

There is no simple answer as to whether it is ethical to take stolen goods from a thief. It may or may not be ethical depending on the human action of the people involved. Still, knowing this will prevent you from mistakenly adopting a straightforward but incorrect rule regarding stolen property.

These systems and guidelines for restitution are in themselves valuable tools for freedom. They are an essential part of the capital structure upon which people build prosperous societies. They are essential because you can think of justice as a healing process, and societies that work to promote it will be self-stabilizing.

Knowledge and resources for implementing restitution make it easier to bring justice to those who need it. But they also help people weigh the risks of things they want to do in the future. Annie may be confident that she can knock a coconut off of your head with a thrown spear. However, the cost of a mistake will be quite high, so she may decide not to attempt it. Evaluating the probability of your plans going wrong is an integral part of protecting liberty and of life in general. All human action is subject to unintended consequences, so it is important to consider the risks.

Murray Rothbard

"Indeed, any actor, when employing means, estimates that he will thus arrive at his desired goal. But he never has certain knowledge of the future. All his actions are of necessity speculations based on his judgment of the course of future events. The omnipresence of uncertainty introduces the ever-present possibility of error in human action. The actor may find, after he has completed his action, that the means have been inappropriate to the attainment of his end."

Risk

A mild storm passes over the island during the night, and when you go out the next morning, the air is crisp and salty. You and Annie decide to spend the day walking around the island to collect wood and other things that may have washed up on the beach. As you travel along the shore, she regales you with stories of the other celebrities that she has met over the years. You can hear the wistful tone in her voice and realize that being away from modern society, let alone high society, has been hard on her.

You wonder if there is something you can do to cheer her up. Having a boat would make her happy, but what about in the short term? One idea that comes to mind is sprucing up her hut. You know she is planning to go to the other side of the island tomorrow, so you would have time to do something uplifting for her. You could weave fresh leaves into the roof, or do a little landscaping around the outside. Maybe even decorate it with seashells.

Then you wonder if that is such a good idea. There is a chance that she might like it, but, then again, she might hate it. It is her personal space, her private property. If you do something to it that she does not like, that could be a violation of the non-aggression principle. It might also make her mad.

To make matters worse, even if you knew exactly what she wanted, there is still a chance you might not execute it properly. You might miss some critical detail or not deliver the right quality of craftsmanship. Despite your best efforts, there is a chance you could fail and cause conflict, like when a barber accidentally cuts a section of hair much too short. Or if someone accidentally bumps into a priceless statue so that it shatters into pieces on the floor.

Annie interrupts your cogitation to ask who your favorite actor or comedian is. After you tell her, she composes herself for a moment and then does a fantastic impression. You smile and laugh but, in the back of your mind, you are less lighthearted. You are beginning to worry that anything and everything you do has a chance to cause conflict. You don't have a perfect understanding of the present, so you can only guess what others are thinking and doing. Even if you knew the thoughts of others, there would still be uncertainty. You would not know if any particular course of action would lead to your intended outcome.

For example, a few days ago, Annie was showing you her juggling skills. She was able to keep five coconuts in the air, but a gust of wind made her lose control. Two of the coconuts collided, and one flew into Big Billy's shoulder. It was an accident, but it was still a conflict. It is bad enough that you cannot always prevent conflict in your little society. What is worse is that you aren't even guaranteed to avoid causing conflict yourself. You realize that with anything you do, something unexpected might happen and lead to conflict. That's true for walking, talking, etc.—everything has some risk. How can you possibly abide by the non-aggression principle if there is no way to guarantee compliance? How can someone who cares about freedom do anything at all without endangering the liberty of others?

Annie runs ahead to look at something in the surf. You walk after her, stepping around piles of stinky, rotting seaweed. When you catch up, Annie shows you a colorful shell, and you start to calm down. You realize there is no perfect certainty for anything, and people usually get along just fine. There is no guarantee that a spear thrown will strike a fish, but Annie has caught many during her time on Danger Island. You can all still make progress toward your goals even if things don't always go perfectly. And, with a little effort, you can still avoid conflict most of the time. The NAP only prohibits causing conflict, not doing something that might cause conflict. The latter would prevent any action at all. You can accept that uncertainty is part of human existence, but the question remains: How should you deal with it in day-to-day life?

Well, people do this naturally all the time. They judge the risks involved in swimming, climbing a tree, and so on, and decide if they are worth it. Each person's risk tolerance is different, and their ability to accurately assess situations will also vary. Fortunately, the world is not so chaotic and unpredictable that people cannot live their lives. Individuals can usually manage to get things done the way they want and achieve their goals. Your chances are good, even if one of your goals is to avoid causing conflict.

You ask Annie what she thinks about taking risks when the outcome is uncertain.

"What, like the first time you kiss someone?"

You grin a little at that, but it seems like a good example. How many young adults have been on a date and wondered if they should go in for a kiss? They want to, but they don't know what the other person is thinking. If the other person wants a kiss, then there is no problem. If they do not, then a kiss might be aggression and result in getting slapped. You could ask for permission, but that might make them lose interest. Risks all around.

"I still remember my first kiss," Annie says. "I was 13 years old. My friends and I were hanging out during the summer and decided to play spin-the-bottle. Let's just say my first spin was very lucky. The rest were okay, too!"

In Annie's game, though, there was virtually no risk of conflict. Just by participating, the other adolescents were giving their consent. In general, things are more complicated. If your goal is to behave ethically, then when you try to decide whether to pursue any particular course of action, you will need to figure out two things. The first is whether you believe there will be conflict. The second is whether you think you will be responsible for the conflict. If you imagine there will not be conflict, then there is no ethical reason to delay. You should not worry too much about sleeping in your own hut or eating your own coconuts. Even if a conflict is likely, that is not a deal-breaker. So long as the conflict will not be your fault, you can proceed with a clear conscience. When you and Annie decided to stand up to Big Billy, that is precisely what happened. Finally, if you foresee that conflict is likely and that you will probably be responsible, then you should avoid that course of action. But not necessarily always.

The NAP says not to cause conflict, so if you were sure that a given course of action would cause conflict, then the NAP would prohibit it. But no such certainty exists, and so a libertarian cannot know ahead of time whether an action will or will not be ethical. Your confidence will vary based on how familiar you are with the circumstances, but you can never be completely sure of what will result. Every action carries some risk of being aggression.

Fortunately, the NAP does not prohibit you from taking actions that only have a chance of turning out to be aggression. You have to use reason and understanding to decide if some action will or will not turn out to be aggression, and then act accordingly. This does not mean that you can ignore the NAP if the consequences are good enough. It only means that because you never know whether any action will end up being aggression, a libertarian is never automatically prohibited from doing any particular thing.

For example, libertarianism prohibits battery. This ethical position is absolutely certain. What is uncertain is whether hitting Annie in the real world will end up being battery in any particular case. So while libertarianism can say, "do not batter Annie", it cannot say, "do not hit Annie" even if it is likely that hitting her will be battery. In a given situation, she might not mind at all.

In terms of your plan to do something nice for Annie, the primary considerations are that she is generally easy-going but also territorial. When it comes to repairing and redecorating her hut, you think that although conflict is not likely, it is not unlikely either. You decide to abandon the plan and try to think of something else. Despite not knowing exactly how to proceed, you are feeling a little better. The conversation has been even more entertaining than usual, and the air has cooled to a pleasant temperature. You have become comfortable with the idea of taking some small risk, but there is still the nagging question of how much risk is acceptable.

It wouldn't make much sense if you couldn't take any risks ever. Everything you do carries some degree of uncertainty, so you would not be able to live if you could not take some risks. But behaving in risky ways a lot of the time will almost certainly lead you to cause conflict. The NAP only says not to cause conflict, so how should a libertarian think about how much risk is acceptable? There is no clear threshold that applies at all times and places. Another difficulty is that you cannot determine ahead of time whether an action will cause conflict. The people involved can change their minds at any time. In general, it seems clear that the risk involved in lighting a candle is acceptably small, even though it could get knocked over and start a fire that burns down your neighborhood. On the other hand, building an unstable bomb is probably not okay, even though it might lead to the same outcome. You know that people would object to one and not the other because the levels of risk are so different.

Candles are just one of many aspects of life that are potentially life-threatening but almost always benign. People expect and are comfortable with the risk involved in lighting one. The additional risk of everyday activities is something they are willing to live with, and expect others to live with, when they cook food, cut down a tree, and so on. This normal level of risk is something that people take for granted and ignore, even though each action has a small chance of causing conflict. It is equivalent to playing Russian roulette with a trillion chambers and only one round of ammunition. Something bad could happen, but it is very unlikely. Every time you do something, it is like pointing that low-risk gun at someone and pulling the trigger.

People should not go around pointing partially loaded revolvers at people and pulling the trigger, but is it always a violation of the non-aggression principle? If someone wants to play the game, then it is not aggression, no matter how brutal the worst-case scenario may be. The players opted in to the game, accepting the risk of conflict.

The day-to-day interactions that people have are like this. They carry some low risk of conflict, and sometimes people accept that risk as a necessary price for cooperation. It is not usually as blatant as a gun, but the risk is still there. So, there are some normal levels of risk that people expect, and taking actions that stay within those limits does not cause conflict. What people consider acceptable will vary between different societies and cultures. Pub-crawling rugby players have a higher expectation of risk from their friends and associates, both on and off the field.

Pulling the hypothetical trigger, then, can be justified based on what people expect, but what if someone expects perfect safety against all the odds? Annie might assume that because you are interested in ethics, you will never do anything that puts her at risk. How can you justify risks in that case? Depending on the circumstances, you can do it in the same way. Even if someone is blissfully unaware of the dangers of going into a situation, they may be responsible for the increased risk they take on. For example, if Annie comes and sits by your fire, you might accidentally stir up some embers that land on her skin and burn her. This hazard is just part of the normal risk associated with sitting around a fire. Annie may not have spent much time outdoors and have little knowledge of camping. But you can hardly be blamed for throwing another log on the fire, even if it increases the danger to those around it. You may or may not be responsible for hurting her if she does get burned. However, despite the increased danger to her sitting near the fire, the risk associated with your tending to it in a standard way would not usually cause conflict.

If you decided to build a fire that had an unusually high chance of burning the people around it, that risk could cause conflict even if nobody actually got burned. The riskiness of an action itself could cause conflict. This is just an input into the same old NAP; there is no separate rule for evaluating the ethics of risky actions. If you believe a risky action was aggression, you would need to show how the risk itself causes conflict. Attempted murder is often aggression, as are many other ways of putting someone's life at risk, but none are necessarily so. You would have to decide on a case-by-case basis.

You spot a long, straight piece of wood tangled in the branches of a bush. Annie helps you pull it free, and the two of you begin to carry it back to camp. Unlike the sun-bleached wood you normally find, this piece is still fresh, and you can smell the sap seeping from the ends. Working together makes collecting wood much easier, but it also slightly increases your risk of conflict. Is that a problem?

Increasing the risk of conflict can cause conflict, but the increase of risk is not necessarily aggression in every case. Just being near another person could increase their risk, and some people might be especially risk-averse. Then again, being near another person might decrease their risk of being mugged, and so on. Risk is a hard thing to predict and measure in general. In acute cases though, like building a bomb in your basement without taking safety precautions, it is easy enough to show the elevated risk levels and prosecute someone for aggression. Such a conflict happens in the present, when the risk level is elevated, even though the larger aggression being risked will happen in the future, if at all.

There will occasionally be times when it is tempting to take large risks. Risks solely to yourself are fine, of course, from the perspective of the NAP. The problem is when extraordinary risks involve other people. The risks may be large in terms of the qualitative magnitude of a potential conflict or the perceived chance of being responsible for it. In either case, putting someone else at greater risk than normal could violate the non-aggression principle. Even if you get lucky and get away without causing some overt conflict, merely putting someone in a risky position is enough. It is like the earlier example of playing Russian roulette with their head, but this time without their knowledge. Stealing is still aggression, even if the victim never finds out. Putting someone in unusual danger is as well.

Conflict-free results do not always justify the means. Take, for example, selling someone an insurance policy that you have no intention or ability to make good on. If your customer never makes a claim, then there is no apparent conflict. But there is a conflict in the praxeological sense. Someone wanted to live a certain way, and you tricked them into something else entirely. That fraud is a real crime, even if the victim never discovers it.

Similarly, it could be unethical for Big Billy to try to murder you, even if he fails. If you know he is trying to kill you, then he may scare you. Scaring someone in this way can be a type of aggression called assault. But what if you do not know about it? Even if you are totally unaware, attempted murder would often be considered a crime in a libertarian society because of the increased risk.

But not always. Big Billy could try to kill you using methods that could never harm you, like simply wishing you would die. If all he does is perform magic rituals to try to kill you remotely, then you may never be at more risk than in ordinary life. If Big Billy were a truly incompetent would-be killer, then he might not be causing conflict even by attempting murder. In an attempted murder, it is exposing a person to increased risk that causes conflict, not the intention.

Risk analysis is not just an essential skill for avoiding conflict in everyday life. It is also necessary for resolving conflicts. Assume you suspect that Big Billy has stolen an ax from you. You think he has hidden it in his hut, and he won't give you permission to go inside and check. You have to decide whether you are willing to go in anyway. You know that if you go in, there will be a conflict. What is not clear is who will be responsible for the conflict. If he did not steal your ax, then going inside his hut would be aggression. If the ax is actually in there, though, then going in there is not aggression and would help resolve a conflict.

In the same way back in modern society, police officers may need to decide whether to break into someone's house. If they believe a crime is being committed, they could save the day. But if they turn out to be wrong, they could end up becoming the criminals from whom they are supposed to protect people. The second case, of course, assumes that nobody is manipulating them. False crime reports have been used to trick the police into unwittingly killing innocent people.

You feel like you may have over-analyzed the situation a little, but, with so few friends, it seems worthwhile to take extra care in keeping them. In the end, you decide to take a safe route and braid Annie a bracelet. There is some risk she might not like it, but there is almost no risk of conflict.

Risk, then, seems to be an inescapable condition of freedom. Protecting liberty does not mean you should always avoid risk. Nor can it be entirely avoided, as some risk is necessary to live: The more people interact and cooperate, the more chance there is of conflict. Nor does attempting to follow the NAP guarantee success. A libertarian could have the best intentions and still cause conflict. You briefly felt doomed by this but, in reality, understanding the NAP and working toward living by it will make you much more likely to find a way to live peacefully.

Your level of uncertainty will be much lower. Specific situations might even call for increased risk to resolve conflicts and protect liberty. Risk is a part of human action, and pursuing freedom requires it to be both mitigated and embraced. Fortunately, there are even more ways for you to reduce the risk involved in both business and everyday life.

Stephan Kinsella

"It is true that a speech act per se is not an act of aggression: It does not intentionally cause the person or property of another to be physically and nonconsensually infringed upon. But some speech acts can be classified as acts of aggression in the context in which they occur because they constitute the speaker's use of means calculated to inflict intentional harm. One clear example of this is threats of force. The threat to stab someone does not actually pierce the victim's skin; it is a 'mere' speech-act, but it is still regarded as aggression."

COMMUNICATION

After some breakfast, you spend the morning making rope from plant fiber. It is hard work, but soon you get into a peaceful rhythm of spinning and braiding. You hope that the rope will be useful for sailing one day, but until then it should help with fishing, gathering wood, and other island activities.

A few hours later, you feel your fingers getting raw. You tie off the ragged end of your project and deputize a rock to watch over it. Then you walk over to sit next to your hut to take a break, eat, and think. Your first thought is that your food supplies are running low. You'll need to devote a few days to restocking before you can spend more time doing other activities like working on your boat. Things are taking much longer than you had hoped.

Disappointed, you lean back on the soft sand. It is comfortable, but you have trouble relaxing because of a nagging feeling that something is watching you. You glance around, but the only thing that seems different is the new wood that you have gathered over the previous few days. Looking at the piles, you take stock of how much you have collected since you were first stranded. You guess that it will be several years before you can build a boat big enough to survive out on the ocean.

Suddenly, you hear a sneeze from somewhere nearby. You look toward the sound, but you cannot see anyone. You are starting to feel paranoid until Annie walks up. It must have been her. You can tell by the way she is holding her spear that she is not happy.

"What's the matter?" you ask.

"Big Billy said he would pay me to guard his hut, but he never showed up with payment," she replies.

Then, from somewhere, you hear Big Billy's voice: "That's because I don't have it yet."

You and Annie look around and finally notice Big Billy. He has buried himself in the sand. Only his head is above ground, but the long, leafy arm of a plant makes it hard to see even that. It is an impressive hiding spot.

"What are you doing down there?" you ask, moving a little closer for a better view.

"Guarding your hut. I'm much stronger than Annie, so I think I can charge more as a guard than her. I'm planning to pay her and keep the difference." he says.

"But I never agreed to pay you to guard my hut," you say. Big Billy takes a moment to consider that.

"On the other hand," Annie says to Big Billy, "you did agree to pay me, so pay up."

Sensing a conflict coming, the part of your brain that has been contemplating ethics sets into motion. Your gut reaction is that Big Billy should pay Annie, but that you don't need to pay him. Is that because of your personal bias, or is it an ethically sound conclusion? How does the NAP apply to this situation? You think about the purposeful behavior involved. In isolation, everything Annie, Big Billy, and you were doing was utterly peaceful and conflict-free. The only interaction has been talking, and the only important thing discussed was what Annie and Big Billy said to each other earlier. The problem seems rooted somewhere in their communication.

How does communication factor into ethical analysis? It is human action like any other, but it is also a tool for avoiding conflict. If you tell people that you are about to chop down a tree, then they can make sure not to get hit when it falls. Communication is also an incredible way to facilitate cooperation, from simple things like sharing tools to complex orchestrations like airplane production. There are many ways that communication can help people to get along. Simply asking for permission before using someone's property can go a long way toward protecting liberty. Telling others what you are doing or planning to do can also help, even if you do not think you are going to cause conflict. Back in modern society, if two people try to walk through a door at the same time, neither will be able to, but a simple "after you" will allow both to pass. However, neither the NAP nor the property system requires you to always ask before using someone else's property. Annie does not mind you borrowing her spear while she is swimming, so you can take it without getting explicit permission every time. Still, even though it is not a requirement, as a practical matter, it makes sense to communicate whenever possible to help protect liberty.

One of the most powerful uses of communication is to make it clear what the ethical implications of future action will be. There are situations where, if you assume everyone involved is in a healthy mental state, then you can take some shortcuts in ethical analysis. For example, if you ask Big Billy to use his walking stick for an hour and he says yes, then you can take it with confidence. You know you will not cause conflict, regardless of whether or not he wants you to use it. You get to skip the work of trying to figure out his mental state. If for some reason he was lying, then any conflict would be his fault because he gave you permission and you would not have used his stick otherwise. This assurance is why communication is such a useful tool for cooperation—it provides some confidence that what you want to do will not violate the NAP.

That said, communication does not mean you are guaranteed not to cause conflict. If you break Big Billy's walking stick, then you will still be responsible. His permission was for regular use and did not give you a blank check to do whatever you like.

Another way to use communication to avoid conflict is to convince others to change what they are doing. If someone is planning to commit a crime, you might be able to talk them out of it. You have done this more than once when it seemed like Annie and Big Billy were going to come to blows. Back in modern society, signs and signals abound that keep people safe and happy or at least help them to avoid disaster. Communication can be beneficial to freedom in many different ways.

Better communication probably would have prevented the hut-guarding dispute, but communication is not some unqualified good. Communication can also be used to cause conflict. A simple example is a threat. When Big Billy first got to the island, he would take whatever he wanted regardless of whom it belonged to. He did not need to physically attack anyone to do it. His massive size made it obvious that he would easily win any fights. His words made it clear that he would employ violence to get what he wanted. Because of this, he did not have to resort to violence to get what he wanted—he only needed to threaten it. A threat was enough to get people to do the things he wanted them to do instead of what they wanted. His threats affected your and Annie's behavior just as much as if he physically held you down. It was coercion through communication instead of physical violence. Similarly, a kidnapper might convince a parent to hand over a large ransom without physically hurting the parent or the child. The kidnapper communicates the intention to hurt the child should the parent not pay. The threat prevents people from doing what they want to do, which means there is a conflict.

Threats are not always aggression, though. When Annie threatened to stab Big Billy a second time with her spear, she was behaving ethically. What makes her threat different? Her words were undoubtedly part of a conflict with Big Billy, but Annie was not the one causing the conflict—he was. Even if she made good on her threat, she would still not have been causing conflict. Annie was only threatening to do something that would not have been aggression anyway. Her warning was intended to end the conflict.

Interestingly, it is not always aggression to threaten someone with aggression, either. If you tell Annie that you are going to murder her, but she doesn't believe you, then it may not cause conflict. She might take it as a joke and think it is funny.

On the other hand, it could be aggression to threaten to do something that is otherwise conflict-free if you had previously agreed not to make such threats. As with physical behaviors, the ethical implications of communication depend on the context.

Communication can cause conflict in other ways, as well. A straightforward example would be telling someone a fruit is edible when it is poisonous. That is not guaranteed to be aggression in every situation, but certainly could be in the right circumstances. A more subtle way was when Big Billy marked one of your coconuts with Annie's initials. In that circumstance, he was communicating that the coconut was hers. When she took it from you, there was a conflict, but the cause was Big Billy's communication. Sometimes the aggression is more serious, as when a con artist defrauds someone out of their property.

Annie might promise to give you two coconuts tomorrow for one of yours today. If, after receiving your coconut, she refuses to give you her two coconuts, then she will have defrauded you. This kind of aggression involves no violence, and you cannot distinguish it from ethical behavior without understanding the communication involved. To an outside observer, things might appear as if you had gifted Annie the coconut, which would have been ethical.

It would also have been fine if she had kept the coconut after explaining her intentions. If she admitted that she was planning to choose later whether or not to return two coconuts, then you could decide if you want to agree to that deal. Instead, she presented one deal and executed another.

Now, what if Annie offers the following deal? You give her a coconut, and there is a 50% chance that she will reciprocate with a fish. If she flips a flat stone to randomly decide whether to provide you with the fish, then she is acting ethically. She is abiding by the agreement to let chance decide the outcome. But if she arbitrarily decides not to give you a fish, then she has initiated a conflict. You agreed to an uncertain outcome based on random chance. You did not agree to let Annie arbitrarily decide whether you would get a fish. In this way, con artists manipulate the odds, presenting early success as guaranteed and inevitable failure later as uncertain and out of their control. The victim will always win small amounts in the beginning and lose big in the end.

So even though lying is not necessarily unethical under libertarianism, it is in certain situations. Gambling would be legal in a libertarian society, but it might be illegal to run a casino that misrepresented the odds in specific ways.

Regarding Big Billy not paying Annie for guarding his hut, Annie and Big Billy had an agreement for a simple exchange. Big Billy did not meet his end of the bargain so, thanks to him, what could have been an instance of cooperation ended up being a conflict. There is no conflict between you and Big Billy though. From your perspective, he was just a creep. He did provide a valuable service by guarding your hut. It was something you probably would have paid for willingly. But that does not mean Big Billy can unilaterally provide the service and determine the price you have to pay. If Big Billy tries to dictate a price and collect a payment, then he is starting a conflict. You are not obligated to pay, and if he takes any money from you, then he is stealing.

You turn to Big Billy to discuss what you have been thinking about, but he cuts you off by shaking his head.

"Save your breath. I know what you're going to say," he says, closing his eyes.

You are a little taken aback since you hadn't finished thinking about it yet.

Annie speaks next, saying, "If you're done being a cabbage, let's go see what you have to compensate me with." She waits for Big Billy to dig himself out of the sand, but he makes no move. "Never mind, I'll do it myself," she says and walks off. Big Billy stays there without stirring, and you start to wonder if he is stuck. You sit back down and keep an eye on him while mulling things over.

You can see how important communication is when dealing with other people. The judgment of the NAP can, at times, depend wholly on what people said. Otherwise-equivalent scenarios can lead to very different outcomes based on a single spoken or written word. What an individual says can change both whether there is conflict and who is responsible.

You wonder why Big Billy's promise to pay Annie is different from other statements of intention, such as, "I'm going to be a scientist when I grow up." You would be surprised if declaring your intended occupation had any ethical weight under normal circumstances, but why is that? To be of ethical importance, the statement has to cause conflict in some way. In Big Billy's case, he got Annie to do something that she would not have done if she had known he was not going to pay her. You can imagine a scenario where he said the same words, but Annie was not interested and instead went for a swim. Then there would not have been any conflict. Similarly, if Annie promises you some coconuts but changes her mind, you might be disappointed, but there would be no conflict. Sometimes a promise can be broken without violating the NAP.

This uncertainty may seem like a problem because people will not always know when a promise will lead to conflict. Making a binding promise can be dangerous. On the other hand, they can be advantageous. People can use them to coordinate their activities, which is good for freedom. Annie will occasionally ask you to give her a boost so she can reach coconuts that are high off the ground. When she promises to share the coconuts with you, the ethical obligation her promise creates gives you confidence that the teamwork will be worth it. You two can achieve things with less risk, which encourages more cooperation than you otherwise would have chosen.

Without the help of communication, ethical problems may seem intractable. The variety of physical situations you could find yourself in can be complex. Communication can also work against you and add another layer of complexity. However, specific types of communication can not only simplify ethical analysis but also make it easier to predict what ethical outcomes will occur in the future. What's better is that situations in which communication can help are relatively common. Consider the following example.

Annie has a coconut, and Big Billy has a fish. If Big Billy gives Annie the fish, and she does not give him the coconut, there is no conflict. Big Billy might want the coconut, but Annie is not obligated to give it to him just because he gave her something. Now, imagine instead that Big Billy says he will give Annie his fish if Annie gives him her coconut. Now if he gives her his fish, does Annie need to give him the coconut? No. Annie never agreed to the exchange, so any conflict over the coconut would be Big Billy's fault.

Now imagine that Big Billy offers the exchange and Annie agrees to it. Is Annie obligated to give Big Billy the coconut now? Still no. If Big Billy never gives her the fish, she will never be obligated to give Big Billy the coconut. When he does, only then will she have an ethical obligation.

So what is happening here? Why do the ethics of the situation suddenly change? It all goes back to human action and the NAP. You know in each case whether Annie is causing conflict without even fully understanding what is going on with each of them mentally. Their physical actions and their communications are enough to create a clear-cut ethical position. This kind of cooperation is so useful that people have developed formal ways of ethically binding actions together. The general framework for analyzing this class of interaction is called a contract.

In general, any time a situation matches this pattern, you can use the contract framework to help you more easily draw ethical conclusions. People of sound mind agree to something and then begin to act upon that agreement. Once you meet the initial conditions, the situation becomes ethically well-understood.

You could, of course, analyze the situation from first principles: understand the human action involved, check for a conflict, and then decide who caused the problem. But sometimes, you can skip all of that by showing that the elements of a contract were in place. There was an agreement, and people took action. Then the people involved will know what their options are, or whether what they did violated the NAP. If someone breaks a contract, then they have almost certainly violated the NAP. As with property, though, contracts are only an approximation of the non-aggression principle. They are beneficial but not guaranteed to lead to the correct ethical conclusion. Whenever the conclusion of the contract framework is at odds with the praxeological analysis using the non-aggression principle, the NAP takes precedence.

As uncomfortable as it was to deal with Annie and Big Billy's disagreement, it did give you some good food for thought. Contracts are unusual because normally the non-aggression principle does not oblige someone to do anything. It only says not to cause conflict. However, a person can choose to enter into a situation where not doing something would cause conflict. That thing becomes an ethical obligation. Creating positive obligations is one reason that contracts are so useful. They are a type of communication that helps people cooperate. Contracts are different from other types of communications because they change the ethical landscape in which people live.

When people cooperate, they sometimes rely on each other to accomplish something. If two people agree to work together, they can achieve things that would not have been possible otherwise. Contracts help because the related parties know that if things do not go as planned, they will be able to seek compensation. Using contracts, you can reduce the risk of embarking on expensive or sophisticated projects with other people. You know that you will not waste your time and resources. As soon as you begin the agreed-upon activity, the other party will either need to comply or compensate you.

Communication is not always perfect. Any time people discuss something, it adds a layer of complexity that can make it difficult to untangle who is responsible for a conflict. Back in modern society, people often use written contracts to make agreements more clear. In this way, contracts are a useful tool for increasing freedom because they help everyone understand what will or will not cause conflict. People can more easily both avoid conflict and more easily resolve it if it does occur. On the other hand, written contracts take a lot of effort to put together and, at the moment, you don't have any paper anyway.

But the piece of paper is not really the contract. The essence of a contract is the agreement between people and the human action in which they engage. Typically, when you think of a contract, you think of some formal exchange of goods or services. But the essence of a contract is a voluntary entangling of human action. Contracts do not need to be in any particular physical form as long as they have the right praxeological elements. Those elements include communication and action. The communication alters who is responsible should a conflict occur, and the action ensures that conflict will occur without some subsequent action. In other words, people say things that create conditional responsibility, and then the conditions are met. Big Billy said he would pay for Annie's services. When she actually provided those services, Big Billy then became responsible for any conflicts over payment.

Back in modern society, people have formalized contracts with rules about what the essential elements of a contract are. The elements are: what is offered, what it means to accept an offer, what intentions the parties had, and the goods and services given in consideration. These legal formalities are useful guidelines for creating contracts and resolving disputes over them, but ultimately the foundation of any contract is the non-aggression principle. People choose actions that ethically restrict their choices in the future. Just as holding a sword over someone's head restricts you from dropping the sword, communication can lead to similar ethical requirements. But only under the right circumstances.

If one person offers and the other person accepts, both can still change their minds. Nothing has changed ethically. But once people begin to engage in further human action based on the agreement, their options begin to change. It might go like this. Offer, no change. Acceptance, no change. Intention, no change. Once consideration is also given, e.g. someone has transferred some item or performed some service, the situation is different. But it is only different because all of the factors are present. Giving consideration alone is not enough. You need all four of these factors to ensure that both the mental and physical components of the underlying human action conform to the contract template.

Contracts are such a powerful tool that some people think that an entire ethical system, or at least a functioning libertarian society, can be built solely on contracts. Unfortunately, contracts are just an expedient. They formalize the process of applying the NAP to certain situations, but cannot function as a complete ethical system. This deficiency should be obvious because conflict can arise without any communication ever occurring.

Unfortunately, no matter how careful you are, even with the most extensive, most detailed contracts possible, you cannot be sure to avoid conflict. Furthermore, people usually do not have time for contracts in all of their day-to-day affairs. So, for someone who wants to abide by the non-aggression principle, what other options do you have? Fortunately, societies have developed many other common patterns of human action that aid people in mitigating conflict. One that is particularly subtle, and hidden in plain sight, is social norms.

Terence Kealey

"The evidence that governments need not fund science for economic reasons is overwhelming, and it is ignored only because of self-interest: The scientists like public funding because it frees them to follow their own interests, companies like it because it provides them with corporate welfare, and politicians like it because it promotes them as patrons of the public good."

NORMS

The next morning you travel into the interior of the island to search for any coconuts that may have fallen overnight. As you walk, you occasionally kick a tree to see if you can shake any loose. Kicking trees is a little dangerous because you never know when a coconut might fall right on you.

After an hour, you find three coconuts that have fallen onto the ground in a bunch. They are a lovely, ripe brown and, when you shake them, you can feel only a slight amount of sweet liquid sloshing around inside. Having eaten so many, you know that these will have soft white meat and a little something to drink as well.

You carry them back to your hut and crack one open. While you eat, you look out to watch the waves. Big Billy is out in the water, but it is not clear what he is doing. He seems to be standing still in chest-deep water, out beyond where the surf breaks. Maybe he is fishing. You should also spend some time today fishing, but you still have contracts on your mind.

Contracts are a great tool to help avoid conflict because they are specific, customizable, and can provide direction in unusual or complex situations. The problem is that they are also slow and laborious. So much so that it doesn't make sense to use them in very common or straightforward situations. The three of you interact in many ways every day, and there is no need for a detailed agreement every time you give Annie a high-five or buy a fish from Big Billy. Some interactions are so straightforward that you would not want to communicate at all beforehand, let alone have an explicit agreement. For instance, you sometimes tap Annie on the shoulder to get her attention.

How, then, can you protect liberty without requiring inordinate amounts of communication before every interaction? Back in modern society, communities naturally solve this problem with social norms. A social norm is a convention for behavior. These conventions increase the amount of work required to avoid conflict in some situations but greatly reduce the amount of work needed in the most common scenarios. This trade-off tends to be a huge win because most people benefit from it most of the time. If you could develop some of those here, it might make explicit contracts unnecessary or, at least, only necessary in certain situations.

As you finish up your coconut, you see Annie swimming in Big Billy's direction. She is a strong swimmer, so you are not too worried about her. As she goes by, she takes a path on the side opposite the island from him, and you realize that this is something that all of you do. Whenever any of you pass someone in the water, you never go in between them and land. It has become a social norm in your little society, having started in your early days on Danger Island, a few weeks after Big Billy got stabbed in the foot.

You remember that on that day, Annie was fishing with a spear, not too far from where Big Billy is now. Big Billy was in the water also, though closer to shore. When Annie was coming back in, he stood up and looked at her. Annie held up her spear and asked him if he was trying to block her from getting back to the beach. He quickly got out of her way. After that, you made a point not to get in her way, either. Eventually, it became an unwritten rule: Don't block someone's path back to land. It is a shared expectation and, now that it exists, it could affect the outcome of ethical analysis.

Similarly, in some places around the world, if you meet someone and they hold their hand out, they expect you to shake it with your hand. You don't need to ask for permission ahead of time, because your new acquaintance already communicated approval by holding his hand out. Another example is that, back in modern society, if you sit down at certain restaurants and order a meal, you are implying that you will pay for the meal once you are finished. The restaurant staff will serve you whatever you like under that assumption. Norms help people cooperate in everyday situations but come at the cost of making it more difficult for outsiders to interact within that society and also for insiders to do unusual things.

Travelers face this problem when they visit cities around the world. On which side of the street do people walk? How do people line up to wait for services? What is the right way to ask for something? When you live somewhere, all of these things seem normal and natural. You know from experience, and this makes it easier to get things done. You have a lot more freedom as a result. When you are a visitor, you have a much harder time trying to do the things you want to do. Not only that, but locals may not even offer the same services and opportunities to someone who does not know how to follow local norms. Then again, sometimes locals have lower expectations of visitors. If a society expects people to do things in a certain way but also expects stupid tourists to do things wrong, then you might have some additional freedom as a visitor.

There is also the question of how norms affect ethical analysis. In the restaurant example, how can the staff be so sure that you will pay at the end of the meal? Is it just them being hopeful that you will decide to honor the bill, or is there some ethical force backing their conviction? It turns out that the non-aggression principle gives weight to social norms, and they can even be the deciding factor when reaching an ethical conclusion.

The reason is that norms can change who is responsible for a conflict. When you walk around on Danger Island, if Big Billy touches you and you don't want him to, then he is causing a conflict. There is so much space on the island that there is no reason for anyone to come into unwanted contact. But back in modern society, there are situations where bumping into others is inevitable. For example, if you ride a train during rush hour, people will likely brush up against you. You may not like that, but it is what happens when you ride a crowded train. If there is a conflict, at least of this variety, you share some blame for getting on the train in the first place.

Norms operate in this way. In wide-open spaces, the expectation is that no one will touch each other without permission. In crowded spaces, the expectation is the opposite. If you enter a society but do not abide by the norms, you will likely be responsible for any conflicts.

Norms can be a factor when trying to save someone's life. At many hospitals, it is normal for someone to try to resuscitate a patient who stops breathing. While at such a hospital, if you stop breathing it will not be an act of aggression for a doctor perform CPR on you, even if you don't want them to. You would instead need to communicate that you do not want CPR, for example with a "Do Not Resuscitate" bracelet. Back in modern society, those who are terminally ill sometimes wear these bracelets in hospitals because of such norms.

Norms are a model of behavior that a person can use to understand the actions of others. They consist of conventions that help people to communicate their preferences. Norms make cooperation much easier, whether you are riding in a taxi or throwing a party. When two people are walking past each other on the street, which side should they pass on? It depends on what people usually do in that particular place. Norms for all sorts of behavior can develop, from what is appropriate to wear to what different behaviors mean. In certain parts of the world, there is one day of the year where boys will playfully whip girls with tree branches, and girls will throw buckets of water on the boys. In other places, either of those things would be aggression. Even where it is acceptable one day a year, doing them would still cause conflict on any other day. But local norms reflect people's expectations. If you are unaware of those expectations, you might be in for a surprise. Worse, you might unintentionally cause conflict.

Annie comes out of her hut and sits on the sand.

"Good morning. Or is it afternoon already?" she says.

"Judging by the shadows, it's a little before noon," you say.

"It's funny, there was a time when I would have paid a lot of money to live like this: drink out of a coconut, swim in the ocean, and lounge around on an empty beach."

"Yeah."

"Now I'd give everything I own just to be back in civilization."

"It may take time, but we'll get there," you say, but you worry it might be a very long time.

Annie crawls back into her hut and, now that you think about it, you realize that some other norms have developed on the island since Annie arrived. If someone wants to talk to you when you are in your hut, and the door is open, they can come to sit in front of the doorway and speak with you. Or you can just shout at them through the walls since the walls don't block sound. Everyone knows that it is okay to do this, and they do not ask permission. If someone wants to sleep or be left alone, they cover their doorway so that everyone knows not to bother them. Something similar happens back in modern society. In many places, it is commonly accepted that you can approach someone's home and knock on the door to get their attention and speak with them. If someone does not want to be bothered, they need to put up a sign that says so.

Norms can develop in societies of any size. The three of you have certain norms, but you and Annie have also developed norms that are specific to your relationship and do not apply to Big Billy. Most of them revolve around the sharing of tools, and the two of you often take for granted that the other might borrow something without asking. On the other hand, while it is normal for you and Annie or you and Big Billy to tap each other on the shoulder to get the other person's attention, Annie has made it quite clear that she does not want Big Billy to touch her.

So, if everyone in a society expects certain behaviors, it changes what actions will cause conflict. That's part of the reason why traveling to a place with a very different culture can be difficult. It is hard to know how to behave appropriately. If you ride a bicycle in a place where people point before turning, failing to do so could cause conflict. Someone might assume that because you did not put your hand out, you are not going to turn, and then move into your path. After a collision, who is at fault? It could be you because of norms.

Similarly, if Big Billy frequently sees Annie borrowing your ax while you are not around, he might infer that it is okay for him to do the same. Assuming there is a conflict, it might be easy or difficult to solve depending on what other communication has happened. If you explicitly told Big Billy that he does not have your permission to borrow tools, then any conflict is clearly his fault. If you never discussed it, or you sometimes granted explicit requests and sometimes denied them, then the answer might require a good deal of investigation and praxeological analysis.

If you wanted to be as sure as possible not to violate the NAP, you could be diligent about asking everyone what they are doing and whether or not what you are planning to do will be a problem. There are many ways that people can communicate, most of which are more explicit than social norms: Text messages, spoken words, and body language are some examples. Unfortunately, that would be comically slow and painfully inefficient. Norms make explicit communication unnecessary, which helps you cooperate with less effort. That is good for freedom.

You see Big Billy wade in from the water carrying some flat, smooth stones. He walks between your hut and Annie's hut along a path toward the center of the island. The trail developed naturally as you, Annie and later, Big Billy, used it more and more to get through the foliage on your way to the other side of the island. Big Billy made his hut further along the path, and you imagine that he is heading there now.

He makes dozens of similar trips throughout the day, and you wonder if he is planning to build a new hut with stone walls. You start to walk back toward his hut and notice that he has paved the path with stones. The craftsmanship is quite good. You enjoy the feel of it beneath your feet and the way it looks winding through the forest. You spot Big Billy and walk over.

"I like what you've done with the path. Are you planning to pave it all the way across the island?"

"Yes."

"That's great. I can't wait to see it when it's done."

"I can't wait to start charging people to use it. My own private road."

"What makes you think you can charge us to use the path?"

"I made it."

"You didn't make the ground, you just paved it."

"You didn't make the ground under your hut, so what's the difference?"

You pause for a moment to think about that. The reason you own your hut is not that you made it. If forces of nature had created the hut, or you lived somewhere like a cave, your ownership would be due to the fact that you started using it without causing conflict. Making it merely gave you the first opportunity to take possession of it. But if you had built the hut on land that someone else was already using, that would have caused conflict. You would not own the hut even though you made it.

"So I think if you built a new path through the woods, then what you said would make sense, but everyone already uses this path to go across the island."

"You weren't using it when I paved it."

"I'm not actively using my hut right now, but that doesn't mean Annie can build a road through it. I'm still using it to store things and as a place to sleep at night. On the other hand, the path is something that we all use. When I'm not walking on it, you can walk on it. We can both walk on it at the same time in different places. And we've all been using it since we got here. The thing that matters is not who is using something but rather what will cause conflict. If you try to stop us from walking on the path that we have been using every day, that's going to cause conflict. If you try to stop us from walking on a new path that you built, that won't cause conflict."

Now that you think about it, was it even ethical for Big Billy to pave it in the first place? If he had done something that interfered with your use of it, then it might have violated the non-aggression principle. Paving the path was compatible with how everyone was using it though, so it seems fine. There are many ways people could use the path without causing conflict.

You realize that public spaces work this way, too. People use an area for a purpose that is not exclusive. Eventually, many people use it for that or other limited purposes, and it becomes understood that the area is public space. Everyone can use it in certain ways without causing conflict. Nobody has exclusive ownership, but you could think of it as everyone having some limited property rights. What is and is not appropriate depends on historical usage and the social norms of those who use it. Shared resources can develop naturally within the libertarian ethical system, and communication and norms can keep everyone living in harmony even without a single person deciding how people use a resource.

In this and many other ways, people use norms to grease the wheels of society. They make the common case the rule and the uncommon case the exception, which leads to greater ease of cooperation. These normal models of acceptable conduct evolve in different ways, and even when societies formally codify them it can be difficult to learn them without immersing yourself in a social group. Still, it is important to do. Failing to account for norms when interacting with others can lead to the same problems and misunderstandings as a language barrier. Getting them right, on the other hand, increases freedom significantly.

It's also important to consider that you cannot solve some ethical problems without understanding the norms involved. If two vehicles are driving in opposite directions on the same side of a road, responsibility for a crash depends on which side of the road vehicles usually drive on. Resolving a fight between two friends is even more challenging because they might have norms between them of which no one else is aware. Moreover, societies are fluid—both the individuals that comprise them and the norms that they develop can change over time. Just like the ever-changing human action of individuals, these unwritten rules form another complex layer in ethical analysis. Their effect on freedom, though, is generally very positive. Social norms are an essential tool in any society, and so humans have evolved to learn and adapt to them.

Though their implicit nature can make it difficult for outsiders to understand what is going on and avoid conflict, they make it much easier for insiders to cooperate. Once norms are understood, they are a means toward greater freedom and can also be the key to resolving specific conflicts.

You now have an additional tool to solve ethical problems. After you decide that a conflict exists, you can use your understanding of norms to help determine who caused it. However, there have been times when you were not sure about whether a conflict exists or who caused it. You wonder if there will be situations where your system for solving ethical problems will break down.

Bob Murphy

"Finally, keep in mind that the ultimate judge in a given case is... the judge. No matter how voluminous the law books, or how obvious the precedents, every case will ultimately depend on the subjective interpretation of an arbiter or judge who must deliver the ruling. We must never forget that written statutes as such are powerless unless used by competent and equitable individuals. Only in a competitive, voluntary system is there any hope for judicial excellence."

AMBIGUITY

Later that day, you get a small fire burning and start cooking some fish. Your neighbors gather around, and it turns into a pleasant evening. Everyone is getting along right now, and it's easy to avoid conflict. You attribute a lot of that to the fact that it is clear who owns what. But what about the *Margit*'s hull? With the NAP, you can solve ethical problems if you understand the human action involved. But what if you don't? With the *Margit*, you don't even know who might be involved, let alone what their human actions are. Who owned the ship before it ran ashore, and what they are doing now? Do they still care about the *Margit*? Are they even still alive?

You ask Big Billy what he thinks.

"Just take it. The thing is probably a hundred years old. Whoever owned it is long gone," he says.

You look at Annie.

"For once, I agree with him. If they wanted their ship, they would have come to get it by now. Who makes wooden boats anymore, anyway?" she says.

Both Annie and Big Billy seem convinced, but you still think it is a tough problem. But what exactly makes it tricky? Solving ethical problems has been reasonably straightforward, at least from a procedural perspective. First, you determine whether or not there is a conflict. If there is, then you determine who caused the conflict. Sometimes it is hard to determine who is responsible for a conflict. But right now, considering whether or not to take the *Margit,* you cannot even decide if there would be a conflict in the first place. Big Billy interrupts your train of thought.

"It's like this. If there is a coconut on the ground, can you eat it?" he asks.

You start thinking about Big Billy's hypothetical, but Annie chimes in.

"We've been over this. You can't just eat something because it's on the ground," she says.

"If I find it in the woods, I can," he replies.

"Only if it fell from a tree. If I am walking through the woods and you see me accidentally drop one of my coconuts, you can't just eat it," she points out.

You suddenly realize that they are both right. There are cases where the answer to Big Billy's hypothetical is yes, and cases where the answer is no. It is an ambiguous problem. The reason is that he did not give you enough information to decide whether there would be a conflict, let alone who is responsible for it. It is just not possible to solve a hypothetical problem that is missing so much information.

In the real world, though, you can spend time getting more information. It may be common for problems to be hazy at first, but they can become clear as new information comes to light. If Big Billy were to come across a coconut on the ground, he could look around and gather more information. He could ask you and Annie to see if anyone dropped the coconut or if it fell from a tree. On the other hand, with a hypothetical problem, you cannot always get more information. It may not be satisfying, but sometimes instead of answering a hypothetical ethical problem, you have to point out that the information given is not sufficient to solve it. This kind of problem is similar to asking how many coconuts you have if you start with three and Annie gives you some more. You can say things about what the answer might look like, but it simply isn't possible to give a conclusive answer to an ambiguous problem like that.

The underlying problem can be illustrated neatly by looking at how it affects the process of resolving conflicts. In general, when solving an ethical problem you first need to understand what is happening, both physically and in the minds of those involved. Once you know what is going on, you can decide whether or not there is conflict, and then finally decide who is responsible for any conflict that exists. Each of these steps requires enough information to make a decision. An ambiguous problem means that some of the critical information for completing one of these steps is missing. If you cannot decide whether there is a conflict at all, you cannot tell if you need to look for someone to blame in the first place. And if you cannot decide who is responsible for a conflict, you can never reach an ethical conclusion. Furthermore, if you have an ambiguous problem and there is no way to get additional relevant information, then that problem is technically known as a deficient problem. You will not be able to solve it no matter how much effort goes into it.

Deficient problems are necessarily ambiguous, but they can be even more insidious than mere simple scenarios that are severely lacking in detail. A deficient problem might have a plethora of information. You might even be able to collect large amounts of additional information to supplement the original problem statement. But as long as the information you start with and everything you collect later is irrelevant, the problem will never be solvable. Big Billy could talk all day about how hungry he felt when he found the coconut, but that won't help you solve the problem.

Another difficulty of deficient problems is that, even if you can gather relevant information, you still might not be able to solve the problem. So long as the amount of relevant information is small, the problem may continue to be unsolvable. For Big Billy's hypothetical, he could add additional information to the problem that is relevant to identifying conflict and its causes. He could tell you how big the coconut is or how close it was to the nearest coconut tree. But it won't matter if none of that is sufficient to solve the problem at hand. He might even tell you who was around, which is usually very relevant to ethical analysis. But if you do not know what they were doing or thinking, then you still won't make any progress.

So, even if he gives relevant information, as long as he does not provide enough to resolve the problem's ambiguity, the problem will still be unsolvable. That's tough because a problem might seem to have lots of information. But if it does not have enough relevant information, then you might just be wasting your time searching through a mountain of distractions. Problems like this are difficult not because they lack information or even because they lack relevant information but because they lack sufficient relevant information. Back in the real world, philosophers sometimes waste their lives analyzing problems that have no solution. To save yourself from the same fate, you need a way of deciding if a problem is deficient or not.

So how can you decide if a problem is ambiguous? First, determine if there is any way to get more relevant information. If there is, then the problem might become solvable after some research. This transition happens all the time back in modern society. Private investigators and arbitration judges gather information until they feel that they understand a situation. Only then do they try to decide what to do.

If there is no way to get more relevant information, then you need to decide if what you have is good enough. But how do you know? It would be useful to have a method of determining when a problem is unsolvable as is. Well, there is at least one method of showing that a problem is ambiguous and not solvable without more information. The technique is to show that adding two different plausible assumptions to it would lead to two different and contradictory ethical conclusions. For example, in a murder investigation, it would be like finding two suspects who had similar motives and access to the victim. You wouldn't be able to decide between them.

To make things a little more abstract, you need to take the original problem and create two new scenarios by adding assumptions. The new problems will be copies of the original problem with some new, carefully chosen information. These problems will have four properties that make them useful for showing ambiguity in the original scenario. First, the new problems must be consistent with the original problem, so the new assumptions cannot contradict anything in the original problem statement. If the original stipulates that the only men were involved, then you cannot assume there was also a woman.

Second, the new problems should lead to obvious ethical conclusions. In other words, the assumption you add to each one should be information that makes it very clear what is going on in that situation. The original problem might be vague or hard to interpret, but your derivative problems should be crystal clear from an ethical perspective. Another way to think about this is that the original problem is difficult to solve, but you are creating new problems that are easy to solve. The murder case might be tricky because two brothers had equally valid motives. For the first derived problem, you might assume that one brother slipped some poison to the victim. Thus, in that derivative problem, it becomes obvious who the killer is.

Third, the new scenarios must lead to contradictory ethical conclusions. The goal is not to generate conclusions that are only slightly different, such as when the same person is guilty but with greater or lesser compensation required. The goal is for the conclusions to be radically different. If one case has the first brother poisoning the victim and the other has the same brother smothering him, you will only show ambiguity about the murder weapon, so this will not be helpful. Instead, one scenario could show the first brother as guilty, and the second could prove him innocent. That level of contradiction hits at the core of the problem.

Finally, the new scenarios must be of equal, high probability. This idea that the new problems are relatively likely is important for showing ambiguity in the original problem. If one of the two is more likely than the other, or if neither of the new scenarios is plausible, then you have not shown that the original problem is ambiguous.

Once you have new scenarios that are consistent with the original, unambiguous, contradictory, and of equally high plausibility, then you have shown that the original problem is ambiguous. The reason is that you have made two equally likely assumptions and received completely contradictory results. Thus, there is no information in the original problem that could lead you to a high-confidence solution.

For example, in Big Billy's hypothetical, the only information is that there is a coconut on the ground and he eats it. You need to construct two new scenarios. In the first, you can assume that the coconut fell from a tree just before Big Billy ate it. In the second, you can assume that Big Billy took the coconut from your pile without asking and put it on the ground. Both of these new scenarios are consistent with the original problem. They are both unambiguous and contradictory—he was almost certainly not violating the NAP in the first one and almost definitely committing aggression in the second. Given what you know about Big Billy and coconuts on Danger Island, both assumptions are equally likely. Furthermore, no scenarios that are more plausible come to mind. Since the new hypotheticals lead to contradictory ethical conclusions, you have satisfied all of the necessary conditions and shown that the problem is ambiguous.

Furthermore, if there is no way to get additional information, then you have also shown that it is deficient. At that point, you can move on with your life. There is no point in thinking about a problem for which you do not have enough information to solve and for which you can gather no additional information. You will never find the correct answer because there is no right answer.

In real life, on the other hand, things are different. For a real-world scenario, there is always a correct answer to any ethical problem. Either there is a conflict or not. That is an objective fact of reality. If there is, then at least one person is responsible. That is also something objective about the universe. However, just because the answer exists does not mean you can necessarily find the information you need to derive it. Even if the truth around the existence of conflict or its cause is not immediately clear, you can usually gather more information to resolve a problem's ambiguity. It might be difficult, especially with things that happened far in the past, but as long as the information still exists somewhere, then, in principle, it should be possible.

But it is not always possible in reality. All of the preceding assumes that you have the time and ability to find the information you need. Even if you could eventually discover the information, sometimes you need to make a quick decision. There may be no time to learn anything new about the situation or circumstances. In that case, you might be forced to deal with a deficient problem in real life as well.

For example, if you see Big Billy about to eat a fish, and you think it might be yours, you need to decide quickly whether to snatch it out of his hands. If it is your fish, then your actions will be ethical. However, if it is his fish, then you will cause conflict. There may be no way to decide with confidence, so you will have to choose based on your estimates and level of risk tolerance. Unfortunately, life occasionally puts people in situations where they need to make split-second ethical decisions.

In a more relaxed setting, you can take your time. You will feel more confident in drawing an ethical conclusion because you can put forth the extra effort to make sure you have enough information. Unfortunately, even in these situations, that is not the end of the story. Even if you are diligent in learning as much as you can, finding the correct solution is still not guaranteed. This uncertainty is because there might always be additional, unknown information that would lead you to a different ethical conclusion.

If you see Big Billy walk over to your coconut stack and look around to see if anyone is watching, you may get suspicious. If he then takes a coconut and runs away, you would be confident that he is stealing it but retrieving his property. If Annie tells you that she saw a strong wind blow the coconut from Big Billy's stack onto yours, you would be confident that he was not stealing it. However, if you then learn that Big Billy stole the coconut before the wind blew it off of his stack, your conclusion will change again. And so on. Given any set of facts about a situation, there is always some additional information that could make a situation ambiguous again or even lead to a different ethical conclusion.

You can take a problem and, by assuming some new information, change the ethical dynamics of the scenario. Additional information can take a problem for which there is no solution and transform it into one that has a clear solution. On the other hand, additional information can take a problem with a clear solution and make it ambiguous. Not only that, but a problem with a clear solution might be transformed into a problem with an equally clear, but contradictory, solution. That is why courtroom dramas exist. New information has the power to completely change the ethical analysis of any scenario and lead to different ethical conclusions.

This instability might be alarming because even with a large amount of true information and perfect logic, you can still come to an incorrect ethical conclusion. Anyone interested in ethical analysis, then, needs to be comfortable with the ideas of ambiguity and uncertainty. No matter how confident you are in your answer to an ethical problem, you must always be open to changing your mind. There is always a chance that some new information could arise that forces you to draw a different, or even opposite, conclusion.

When trying to gather information to solve an ethical problem, you can use the same technique of generating scenarios and comparing how useful they seem. By exploring how various assumptions change the ethical landscape, and by evaluating how likely they are, you can decide which avenues of investigation are worth pursuing.

That said, if you wanted to maximize your chances of arriving at a correct conclusion, you could spend forever gathering information. This, however, would lead to a bad situation where conflicts never get resolved, which seems worse than making riskier decisions on less data. The question becomes: When do you know that you have done enough research?

Understanding of the world and practice with ethical problem solving will help you know when to draw an ethical conclusion. This wisdom will allow you to balance the risk of incorrect outcomes with the need to resolve conflicts as soon as possible. Resolving a conflict is urgent because the longer a conflict goes unresolved, the further the world moves from the libertarian counterfactual.

You decide to apply this method to the long-standing problem of the *Margit*. You have been keeping an eye on the old ship for some time now but have not seen signs of anyone who might be using it or interested in coming back to claim it. You haven't seen hints of any new people at all. While the owner might still be using it, you think it is much more likely that they abandoned the ship. You are not perfectly certain, but nothing in life can be, so you decide to move forward.

"All right, everyone," you say. "Tomorrow I have a job for you."

Leonard Read

"Lost and adrift on a raft for days, a man might offer his fortune in exchange for a hamburger. Yet, the same person, following a lusty meal, might not offer a penny in exchange, though the hamburger had changed not at all.

  "Individuals have varying value judgments. Value in the market sense, therefore, is a subjective rather than an objective determination. In a way, it is like beauty. What is beauty? It is what you or I or other individuals think is beautiful. It depends on subjective or personal value judgments, judgments characterized by constant variation.

  "Value, as beauty, cannot be objectively determined. That all persons may think of a certain sunset as beautiful, a given monster as hideous, gold as desirable, or mud pies as useless does not alter the fact that these are subjective judgments. Such unanimity merely asserts that some subjective judgments are similar."

LIFEBOAT SCENARIOS

The next day, you head north to dig out the *Margit*. Annie comes along to help, and you pay Big Billy a fortune to get his assistance as well. You set out in the morning with some wooden poles and partial coconut shells for scooping. The work is slow, and soon the sun on your back feels as heavy as the sand you're excavating. The three of you work hard for hours, and you start to worry that you're not making enough progress. If things take too long, the tide will eventually come in and destroy all of your progress.

After eight hours, the waves are beginning to creep back toward where you're working. You have dug a deep trench around the ship. In some places, you could dig no further because water would seep into the hole. Most of the sand that was inside the hull has been scooped out. You call everyone together on one side, and the three of you start pushing. With your help, the weight of the *Margit* overcomes the remaining sand, and it rolls flat onto the beach with a thud. Annie props a pole against it to keep it from sliding back into the hole.

You step back and drop to the ground, exhausted. Then you look it over. Now that it is above ground, you see that while some parts of it are well preserved, others have rotted badly. You worry that you may have wasted everyone's time.

There is a large hole in the sand where the ship used to be. It has already begun to fill slowly from the bottom with water. You imagine it will not take long before the beach has reclaimed the cavity. After catching your breath, you walk back over to inspect your prize up close. The outside is a patchwork of boards, some of which are suspect in quality. You decide to check on the interior as well.

Aside from some rotten rope, you see little remaining inside the ship. You lethargically go about removing the remaining sand and seaweed. To your surprise, you find some buried treasure. It is not gold or rubies but something even more valuable for people stranded on an island: a miraculously unbroken bottle of rum.

You hold it up to the sun. The glass has become rough and opaque over time, and the way the light glistens through it makes you wonder how far it traveled to come here.

You pay a second fortune, including the only rum on the island, to get Big Billy to help you and Annie drag the *Margit* up the beach and into a clearing where you will be able to work on it without it being washed away by waves or buried again in the sand. The three of you are already weak from digging, so the short trip lasts much longer than you expect. When you finally finish, you take a hard look at the old ship and wonder if it will ever sail again.

Then you wonder if Big Billy is going to open Danger Island's first bar. You turn to suggest the idea to him and watch as he chugs the last of the rum. He is a big man, but you estimate his chances of surviving all of that alcohol to be no better than even. He takes a few unsteady steps toward the water. With a growl, he lurches forward in an attempt to throw the bottle against some of the beach rocks. He misses wildly, and the bottle sails out into the waves. He looks like he is going to yell at the ocean, but he suddenly stops and then turns away with confusion in his eye. Annie wades in after the bottle and brings it back. Big Billy vomits and then collapses dangerously close to the surf.

"I thought there might be a little left, but it's all saltwater now," she says, pouring out the bottle while soaked with seawater herself.

"We could use it to store water, at least," you say.

"Let's use it to send a classic message in a bottle. You know, just in case. At least someone might know our story," she says.

The two of you sit to discuss what to write. After a while, you notice that the waves are starting to lap up against Big Billy without waking him from his vegetative state.

Annie asks if the two of you should help him. You think the answer is obvious—of course you should. Big Billy can be a problem sometimes, but ever since Annie put him in his place, he has mostly been helpful. Then again, if this had happened the first day he was here, you would have been tempted to leave him to drown. Would that make you a murderer? Back then, people might understand that helping him would only lead to more conflict and misery for you and Annie. What about now, though? If you just left him there that would be bad for the economy, but would it be unethical?

You struggle to find any potential conflict. Big Billy is lying there, and you are sitting over here. Moreover, even if there were a conflict, how could it be your fault? There are no agreements about this kind of situation. Nothing like this has ever happened before, so there aren't any norms either.

It seems like you are ethically in the clear to let him die, but even if there were no benefit to keeping him around, you feel like saving him would be a good thing to do. It's a moral impulse and something outside of ethics.

Ethics and morality are independent evaluations of human interaction. A wealthy business owner who donates money for medical research might be doing something good and ethical. A person who drinks too much, passes out on the beach, and puts himself in mortal danger might be doing something bad but ethical. If you hear about someone poisoning their parents, that may be both bad and unethical. If someone steals from a rich person and gives to a poor person, that would be unethical, but some people would consider it to be good.

You find it a little disconcerting that people might consider unethical actions to be good. What is reassuring, though, is that aggression can never be unanimously good. It might seem good to some people, but any aggression will always have someone who considers it to be bad, namely the victim.

The non-aggression does not prohibit all bad behavior, and it does not require that you do good things either. Luckily for Big Billy, you think saving him is a good thing and something you should do. From a practical perspective, the more people, the better. Even Big Billy, who sometimes causes problems, is a net benefit to your little society. He produces a little more than he consumes. He occasionally has something interesting to say. You are not sure you could have got the *Margit* out of the ground without him. But it's not just that he is useful. He's a person whose life has been difficult, and you can relate to that. You want freedom for yourself and everyone else as well. And if Big Billy dies, he won't be able to do the things he wants to do. He won't be able to do anything at all. Death is the end of freedom. You wouldn't want it for yourself, and you don't think Big Billy wants to die either. You get up, walk over to him, and lift his head just as a wave rolls by.

Your muscles are already tired from digging and moving the *Margit*, so moving Big Billy ends up being a literal pain in the butt. After a few days, both your exhaustion and Big Billy's hangover wear off, and attention returns to the possibility of leaving the island. For weeks, it is all anyone can talk about. The *Margit* was no longer seaworthy when you pulled it out of the sand, but repairs have been going well. You have enough wood stockpiled that you think you will be able to fix it. You quickly find out that what you need most is tree sap for making glue and sealant. The process is slow and uncertain, but over time it becomes clear that the *Margit* will return to the ocean. Annie and Big Billy spend more and more of their time looking for, collecting, and cooking sap. A few weeks later, you are physically drained, nearly bankrupt, and ready to launch the ship.

With repairs completed, you start to worry less about keeping the ship afloat and more about having enough food and water once you are out at sea. During the day you craft water containers, and at night you work on splicing grass blankets into sails. Eventually, you have enough food, but you end up waiting for an extra week to gather enough fresh water.

You estimate that you have enough supplies to last three months on the ocean. More, if you can catch some fish or collect rainwater along the way. A heavy storm would be a real problem, though. The *Margit* will have enough trouble holding together on a calm ocean, let alone violent swells.

You charge Big Billy a fortune for passage on your ship, but he recently came into a lot of wealth and seems eager to get off the island. The three of you spend a few days loading almost everything you own onto the *Margit*. It seemed so big when you were moving it across the land. Now, with all of your cargo, it seems small and cramped.

You look around one last time at what used to be your camp to see if there is anything else you would like to bring. It seems as if you have taken care of everything. Well, except for one thing. Annie still has not sent a message in her bottle. You walk over and ask her about it.

"I don't know what to say. We don't know where we are, so we can't ask for help. We only have this peeled bark to write on, so there isn't enough room to say much of anything."

"Just write the most important thing," you say.

Annie gives you a look but then seems to consider what that might be. She writes a short message and slides it into the bottle.

"How are you going to cap it?"

"I picked up the cork off of the beach after I pulled the bottle out of the ocean. Hopefully, it will last long enough for someone to find it." Then she seals the bottle and wades out into the ocean.

You have all become very familiar with the beach and the currents around it, so you know exactly where she is heading. A little way out, there is a shallow sandbar that has a strong current next to it. When she gets there, she almost looks like she is standing on water, and you watch her hurl the bottle out into the waves.

When she gets back, you say, "I was thinking that maybe we should have wrapped the bottle in something colorful to make it easier to notice."

"Too late now."

You shrug and ask, "What did you end up writing?"

"I'll tell you if we survive this sea voyage."

You laugh, and the two of you go back to the *Margit* to continue preparations.

With everything ready to go, the anticipation builds as you wait for a clear and calm day to launch. When that day arrives, the excitement continues to grow as you delay a bit longer for the tide to be just right. With your little ship complete and loaded with cargo, the three of you gather to take one last look at the island. Annie winks at you and then turns to Big Billy.

"Are you sure you want to go back?" she asks. "If you come on board you'll have to follow the rules, but if you stay here on the island, you will be able to do whatever you want. You'll be king of the island."

"King of the island," he repeats. Big Billy thinks for a moment, his eyes drifting between the island and the sea. Then he gets a serious look on his face, and you know he has made his decision.

"It would be good to be king," he says, "and I'm not too confident in this boat. But what I really want are some blueberry donuts. No, I have to risk it."

"What about you, captain?" Annie asks. "It might be a lot safer with fewer people on board."

"We have a better chance of making it if we work together. Just look at this ship," you say, nodding at the *Margit*. "I couldn't have done it without you. Both of you. Whatever happens, let's face it together."

You look at your old camp and think about all of the progress your little society has made since you came to Danger Island. You worked hard, acquired capital, and found ways to get along. Now, as you prepare to depart, you feel a little sentimental about what you are leaving behind. But you are also proud. You started with very little and turned the island into a much better place to live. You worked hard and built so much to make your lives easier. Now you are going to give it all up for a chance at something more—an opportunity to get back to the modern world.

Yet you do have one nagging reservation. On the island, you have enjoyed a lot of liberty. As Annie pointed out, once you return to modern society, you will likely have less of it.

You will lose some liberty by going home, but the infrastructure, economy, and other capital will be so much better. Not to mention reuniting with all of your friends and family. The additional capital still seems worth it, but there is a real trade-off to consider.

You have done so much here but, back in modern society, you will be able to do even more. The resources, tools, equipment, and services available will multiply your productivity. You will be able to earn more money in an hour than you used to make all day. You will be part of a vast division of labor that produces incredible amounts of capital. Your standard of living is going to skyrocket. You are going to have access to so many goods and services. You only have to survive this journey on the ocean, and then you will be back. You can hardly wait.

You load up the last of the supplies and wait for the tide to roll in. When the water is high enough, the three of you roll the *Margit* on wooden logs until it reaches the waves. After that, it becomes a struggle to move the ship with each swell until it stops scraping along the sea bed. Finally, it is deep enough, and the three of you climb on board. You seem to go nowhere for a few agonizing minutes, but then a current pulls you along the beach and out away from the island. The waves rattle the ship but, eventually, you make it out to calmer water.

Looking back at the island, it seems smaller than you thought. Later that day, Annie shouts that she sees another island in the distance but, when you look, it is too hazy to be sure. You try to steer the *Margit* in that direction, but none of you are skilled at sailing a ship like this, and your rudder and sails are so rudimentary that you aren't sure it would matter anyway.

The excitement slowly wears off, and all that is left are the endless blues of ocean and sky. The three of you eat your first meal at sea, and Annie sings a few songs to pass the time. The sun sets more quickly than usual, and you hold the rudder steady toward the fading light. As night comes, you try to focus on a few stars that start to glow ahead of you. Later in the night you look up at the constellations and wish you knew more about astronomy. Then you could figure out exactly where you were on the planet and pick the best direction to sail. Instead, you curl up in some grass blankets and try to stay warm.

You spend the next few days fishing with varied success. Some days you can't seem to catch anything. Other days, the fish seem to be everywhere. One day Big Billy says he sees a whale, but when you go over to look, you don't see anything. Perhaps because his large frame partially blocked the view. The cramped quarters of the boat make Big Billy even more intimidating than he was on the island. He is tranquil now, but how long will it last?

A few days later, Annie tells you that she saw some sharks while you were asleep. You stare over the side of the boat and wonder what else is down there in the deep.

The weather is generally favorable, but occasionally the winds pick up and toss the *Margit* around. Each time, the ship holds together but you worry about leaks. You ask everyone to keep an eye out for moisture inside the hull. You're not sure what you can do to plug any holes, but whatever the problem is, it will be better to catch it early.

Big Billy slumps down against the bulwark and moans. He seems seasick. After a few minutes, he says, "What are we going to do if the ship sinks?"

"We would have to swim for shore," you say. "Though it might take a long time. We haven't seen anything that even vaguely resembles land in days."

Big Billy looks around and says, "What if the ship sinks and we have to swim really far and we get tired. And when everyone is about to drown from exhaustion, a single wooden log drifts by, but it is only enough to hold one person?"

"I guess whoever grabs it first would get to use it," you say.

"But what if we all grab it at the same time?"

"I guess we would all drown," you say dismissively.

All that follows is a depressing silence. You try to lighten the mood.

"Don't worry about the ship. The *Margit* will hold together. We made it through that wind and rain a few days ago, so we should be all right. You'll see."

"But what if we run out of food?" Big Billy asks.

"Then we will have to hope the ship holds together, because we won't have the energy to swim," Annie says.

"This is serious."

"We are not going to run out of food," Annie says.

"Why not?"

"Because you have the smallest food reserves, so you will run out first. Then after you die, we are going to eat you."

Big Billy looks angry for a second, but only grunts and closes his eyes to think. Then he opens them wide and says, "You can't eat me. I don't give you permission to eat me."

"Of course, we're not going to eat you *now*," Annie says playfully. "That would be criminal. But after you are dead, it won't cause a conflict." She looks at you and says, "Right?"

You think about it for a few moments. Then you ask Big Billy what he wants to happen to his coconut opener when he dies.

"I want to leave it to my mom."

"And what about your bandanna?"

"I want to leave it to any children that I might have, so they have something to remember me by."

"Do you have children?" Annie asks.

"No idea," he says.

"O-kay," you say. "Well, my point is you could leave your body to someone when you die. Then they will own it. If you make a deal with them ahead of time, then maybe your body won't get eaten, and we can all relax."

Big Billy stares at you blankly. "Why would you have to honor our agreement after I am dead?" he asks.

"You can make it a deal, like a contract. You give me something in exchange for a service. It's like prepaying for funeral services. Just because you're dead doesn't mean the undertaker doesn't have to hold up his end of the bargain."

"What if the undertaker dies?" Annie asks.

"What do you mean?"

"Well, if you make a deal with the undertaker, but he dies before you do, what then?" she says.

You think about that for a while. Some deals simply cannot be completed if one of the parties dies. Does that lead to conflict? In some cases, it probably does not. If you pay someone for the right to buy their home, but the home burns down before you exercise that right, that does not cause a conflict. In other cases, it could. If you knew you were going to die soon, and you took payment for a job far in the future, that is blatantly fraudulent. This question could be made clear with explicit death clauses in every agreement, but most of the time, it is better to rely on norms and customs.

Death does not erase all ethical considerations and, in retrospect, that shouldn't be surprising. Murder is a crime even though the victim isn't around to complain about it. Conflict is not just the pain and suffering of the victim. It is the clash of human action that occurs while they are alive. Just because they are gone does not mean that the conflict never happened. Their death does not alter the fact that justice would lead to a very different world.

If someone stole something from your friend, it would be ethical to recover that item even after your friend's death. Similarly, it is ethical to pursue other kinds of restitution after someone meets their demise. Death does not change the fact that the world differs from the libertarian counterfactual. Death only makes justice that much harder to achieve.

Ethical considerations survive not only the death of a victim but the death of a criminal as well. If Big Billy throws a rock at Annie and hurts her, it may be evident that Big Billy has initiated a conflict. But what if Big Billy dies before the rock hits her? Is there still a conflict? If so, what actions are colliding?

Human action is purposeful behavior. A rock does not have any intentions, but when Big Billy throws it through the air, the behavior it exhibits is purposeful. The purpose is that of the thrower. In this way, the physical component of human action can be separate from the actor in time and space. Setting off a remote explosion can cause conflict whether it takes the signal a few nanoseconds or a few years to reach the detonator. It is still part of human action whether the actor is still alive or not and, in the same way, the actor is still responsible for the action whether or not they are still around to answer for it.

Just as people can bind each other with contracts while they are alive, those contracts do not necessarily end when a person dies. If you hired Annie to protect your family and paid her in advance for five years of service, she would not be off the hook if you died. On the other hand, there are also cases where an agreement would be void. If someone pays you to be their physical trainer for a year but then dies, then obviously you cannot complete the remainder of the contract. You are not sure which case Big Billy's body falls into, but the idea should keep him from getting too worked up and causing trouble. You tell him that the agreement will still hold.

"Okay, I leave my body to you if you agree not to let Annie eat it."

You agree, and he begins to calm down. You will have to caution Annie against teasing him, especially if his food reserves really do run low. Boredom has been a real problem though, and you can see why Annie would want to liven things up. For the moment, however, you prefer to relax to the natural sounds of the ocean after the tense and heated discussion.

Out on the ocean, there is not much to do, so you have a lot of time to think. The only real work is managing the sails and the rudder. You are not sure where the closest land is, but you have been heading west as best you can. Every night, you look around to try to see the lights of ships or cities. The first few times you thought you saw something, it ended up being a low star or the moon peeking above the horizon. Every time you thought you saw land, it was just the shadow of a cloud, a patch of seaweed, or something else. You've been wrong so many times that you probably would not get your hopes up unless the ship ran aground.

One night while Annie is sleeping, Big Billy comes over to you and whispers, "I have a question."

"What is it?"

"If you had to pick between one person dying and three people dying, which would you choose?"

"One."

"Right, good. So we're probably going to be out on this boat for a long time and food is going to run low. We'll all starve to death. That's bad."

"That would be bad."

"But if one of us died, then there might be enough food so that the other two could make it to safety."

"That's possible."

"Okay, then we need to kill Annie and take her food."

You pause a moment. "Why shouldn't you be the one to die?"

"That wouldn't make any sense. I have the least amount of food. Our best chance is with Annie."

"I'm not going to murder Annie."

"No, of course not. I can take care of it," Big Billy says, unconsciously rubbing the scar on his foot.

"I'm not letting you do it either." Not to mention that with Annie out of the way, you doubt you could prevent Big Billy from eating your food as well.

"But you said one is better than three."

"Yes, but you can't violate the NAP to get a better outcome."

"Even if something was going to destroy the whole world? What is the point of an ethical system that gets everyone killed?"

"You don't know that we are going to die."

"But if you did know, what then?"

"Then we'd have to ask Annie how she felt about it. If she is okay with dying to save us, then it is ethical."

"So she gets to decide if we live or die? How is that fair?"

"I guess we all would equally have the option to die to save the others. And if none of us choose to do that, we can hardly blame the others for making the same decision."

"And if only Annie could save us? You can't sacrifice the majority for the sake of the minority."

"If Annie ends up being the only one with food because she saved the most and ate the least, why should we get to eat it and not her? What Annie wants to do is her decision. We might disagree with her choice, but it is up to her whether it is better to sacrifice herself or not."

Big Billy wrinkles his brow and slinks away. You wonder if he is planning to make a similar offer to Annie. She'll refuse, you think. Probably.

The next day while the others attempt to fish, you continue to worry about your dwindling food supplies. Big Billy lacks impulse control and will often eat more than he needs to. Annie is right that his supplies are going to run out first.

There are occasionally fish to catch in the sea, but they are an unreliable food source. Sometimes a bird flies by, but Annie has not been able to trap one yet. She spends a lot of time thinking about how to use fish scraps as a lure, but so far none of the birds have noticed, or, at least, they haven't taken the bait.

While Big Billy is certainly free to use his property as he sees fit, you worry that when his savings run out he is not going to waste away peacefully. He is going to see your food and Annie's food and convince himself that he should have some of it. You decide to have a private talk with Annie about how to handle that eventuality.

Later that night, Big Billy falls asleep, and you motion for Annie to come over for a quiet conversation. You explain that you want to prepare in case Big Billy runs out of food. You tell her that you are willing to share some of yours, but you want to ration it and make sure he doesn't squander yours as well.

"He might not like being put on a diet. What if he tries to eat more than you are willing to give him?" Annie asks. She thinks for a moment, unconsciously rubbing the scar on her foot. Then she says, "Why don't we take care of the problem before it starts?"

You think about that. If you knew that Big Billy was going to attack you, it might justify some action against him. Then again, if he were not going to attack you, then your preemptive attack would be aggression.

"We would probably be the villains in that situation," you say.

"Okay, so why don't we do this? I will poison his water supply, but then before he can drink it, you dump it out into the ocean. If I know Big Billy, he'll start drinking seawater and dehydrate himself to death."

"How is that not murder by another means?" you ask.

"Well, he never drank the poison, so I didn't kill him. You saved his life by preventing him from drinking poison, so you didn't kill him either."

Her argument sounds superficially plausible, but it makes you suspicious. If she is right, then you could kill anyone that way with a clean conscience. It seems like the method should not have such a big influence on the ethics. These strange scenarios are difficult to think about, but they help you test the ethical system that you have adopted. They gauge the quality of the ideas.

When there is a difficult ethical problem like this, it is sometimes helpful to try to come up with an ethically equivalent scenario that is easier to understand. For example, in this case, you might think of Big Billy riding on a train. There are two switches along the track, both of which are currently set to send Big Billy in a safe direction. That is unless someone uses them to switch the track. If that happens on either switch, then the train will crash, and Big Billy will die.

In Annie's hypothetical, death by poison is the first switch. Annie flips that when she puts poison in his water. The second switch is dying of thirst. Annie switches that one too since even if Big Billy discovered the poison in his water and did not die of poisoning, he still would not have any water to drink.

When you dump out his water, you are flipping the first switch back to the safe track. So Big Billy won't die of poisoning. But he will still die of thirst when his train reaches the second switch. Then Annie would still be guilty of murder. You explain this to Annie, and she looks deflated.

"So what do we do?" she asks.

"When his supplies start getting low, we'll sleep in shifts. I imagine he would try to steal before attacking us. If that happens, then we can take action."

Annie seems satisfied with that and sits back to listen to the sound of waves gliding around the sides of the boat.

"This rule of yours seems way too rigid sometimes. What if there is an emergency and it makes sense to bend the rules temporarily?"

"Can you give me an example?" you ask.

Annie thinks for a minute and then says, "Let's say that Big Billy throws a spear at you and the only way to defend yourself is to block it with my coconut opener, which happens to be right next to you."

You look at Annie's coconut opener, which happens to be right next to you.

"You know that if you don't use my coconut opener, you will die, but if you do, then you will be fine. Is it ethical to take it?"

"I imagine that if Big Billy were attacking me, you wouldn't mind at all if I used it to defend myself."

"However," she says with a wave of her hand, "let's just say you know that I don't want you to touch my coconut opener under any circumstances. For some unfathomable reason, I'd rather the spear kill you. Are you willing to die for your philosophy?"

"If you won't let me borrow a rock to save my life, I think the problem is with you, not the philosophy," you say.

"Okay, but don't dodge the question. What if instead of the coconut opener you have to pull me in front of you? Either you die, or I die." Her tone is playful, but she has a point.

"The answer is the same—it's up to you. I think most people wouldn't blame you if you didn't want to die on my account, but if you did, then it would be okay for me to pull you. Otherwise, it isn't. Most people would think poorly of you if you wouldn't let me use the rock. They would say you are not a good person, not moral. But, in terms of ethics, who are they to say what is more important? I might think a rock is trivial compared to my own life, but that's just my opinion. It's subjective, so only you can decide."

"So you would die."

"Well, there might be some social norms that come into play."

"Assume there aren't any."

"It also depends on whether I had time to think about it. In your situation, I might instinctually use the rock to save myself. Then the only purposeful behavior would be Big Billy's, and he would be to blame."

"So you could only save yourself if you did it unconsciously? That doesn't make sense."

"Well, I wouldn't be doing anything really, just reacting reflexively to Big Billy. It's only when I engage in purposeful behavior that I might violate the NAP."

"Okay, assume nothing is forcing you into it in any way."

"Then I guess my only options would be to violate the NAP or die, and the only ethical option would be to die. Maybe some things are worth dying for."

"A rock?"

"A principle."

Annie doesn't pursue the idea any further, but you wonder if there are situations where you might ethically be able to direct aggression away from yourself. If Big Billy said he was going to kill either you or Annie and he said you could pick which one, would it be ethical to pick Annie or does libertarianism force you to choose yourself? If you were to pick yourself, there would be a conflict between you and Big Billy, but you would not be responsible for it even though you picked yourself—he is. Similarly, if you were to pick Annie, you would not be responsible for any conflicts among the three of you because you had no real control over Big Billy. If you had any real control of the situation, you would have prevented him from causing any conflict at all.

Certainly, convincing him to attack Annie when he had no intention of hurting anyone would be unethical. But if he is already coming after you and only you, what then? If you get him to attack Annie instead, does that violate the NAP? Like all ethical questions, the circumstances could lead to either conclusion. If you pull Annie in front of you so that she suffers Big Billy's attack, then you would be causing conflict. If you jumped behind her in the hope that she could protect you from Big Billy, perhaps you would not be causing conflict. Not exactly heroic on your part, but not necessarily unethical either.

At least, that is the way it seems, but you've learned to be cautious about jumping to conclusions when analyzing ethical problems. It is deceptively simple: Ethics is all about identifying conflict and its causes. Then again, ethics is ultimately about helping people get along so they can have a good life. Strangely, the hardest part of being out on the ocean have been the ethical questions that have come up. They have been difficult, but they have also helped sharpen your thinking. These kinds of problems might even be the best way to test the limits of, and improve upon, an ethical system. Hopefully, all of this work will help the three of you on the remainder of your trip, however long that may be.

Henry Hazlitt

"The capitalist system has lifted mankind out of mass poverty. It is this system that in the last century, in the last generation, even in the last decade, has acceleratively been changing the face of the world, and has provided the masses of mankind with amenities that even kings did not possess or imagine a few generations ago."

CAPITALISM

After weeks of nothing but wind and waves, Annie spots an island in the distance. As if that were not exciting enough, a few hours later, you are elated to see a speedboat approaching. Annie tells Big Billy to get under one of the blankets so that they don't see his bandanna and worry that your ship is a pirate ship. Big Billy does so grudgingly. Annie smiles at you and winks.

Annie looks ecstatic to have found civilization, but you notice her holding her spear just out of sight as the speed boat pulls up along your starboard bow. The young woman at the helm looks over your ship with a smirk.

She says, "Hello there. My name is Chelsea. Allow me to welcome you to Freeport. We tried to radio you, but from the look of things you didn't bring one." Big Billy snorts under the blanket, and Annie puts her foot on him as a warning. Chelsea continues, "Things work a little differently here, so I am going to give you the basic information you need. Do you understand?"

You and Annie both nod.

"Wonderful. Freeport is that nice city over there." Chelsea jabs her thumb over her shoulder. "We get visitors from all over the world, so please be respectful of the people you meet, even if they are strange.

"I work here as a security officer. People with my job wear this symbol," Chelsea says, pointing to a patch on her shoulder. "There are different security companies in Freeport, but officers from any company will help you if you ask.

"The laws are super simple here. No assault or battery. Don't hurt or threaten anyone. No theft. Don't steal anything, and respect people's property. That's the majority of it. Does that make sense?"

You and Annie both nod.

"If you choose to enter the city, you must abide by those rules. Do you agree?"

"That seems simple enough," Annie says.

"Simple, but not easy. Like diet and exercise," Chelsea says. "Just so we are clear, when I say don't hurt people and don't take their stuff, that includes derivative crimes like extortion, trespassing, and fraud. Okay?"

"Okay," Annie says.

"This sounds like the non-aggression principle," you say.

"That's right," Chelsea says. "Freeport is a libertarian society, so follow the non-aggression principle while you are here."

"Okay," you say.

"Great. A little ship like yours can dock at Pier Three for free. Any yellow roads throughout the city are also free to use. There is a market near Pier Two where you can buy anything you need. If, against all evidence to the contrary, you are here on holiday you can find the tourist center near Pier Four. Any questions?"

"How many people live here?" Annie asks.

"Oh, we just passed five thousand," Chelsea says. "That's permanent residents. When the weather is nice, we usually have a few hundred visitors as well."

"Where is this place?" you ask.

Chelsea laughs. "Wow, you really are lost at sea, aren't you? We are somewhere between Madagascar and Sri Lanka," she explains, "but don't let the location fool you. Freeport is one of the best places on Earth."

You try to remember what islands this size exist between Africa and India, but you can't think of any.

"If Freeport is so great, how come I've never heard of it?" Big Billy says, still under the blanket.

"Is that a ghost or can your ship talk?" Chelsea asks.

Annie moves off of Big Billy, and he stands up. Chelsea looks him over without changing her expression. Then she says, "Well, why don't you stay awhile and find out? Just a few questions first. Are there any other people on this ship?"

"No," Big Billy says.

"Where did you sail from?"

"Danger Island," Big Billy says.

"I guess your hometown isn't that famous either since I've never heard of it. You're not flying a flag; where is your boat registered?"

"We don't know," he says. "We found it on the beach. Law of salvage."

"We had to take it," Annie says. "We were stranded."

"Uh-huh. And how did the three of you end up stranded on this island?" Chelsea asks.

"We don't know. We never met before." Big Billy says.

Chelsea raises an eyebrow but finally says, "All right, let's treat this as a search and rescue operation. I'll let people know you are coming, but, since you're not in any immediate danger, I won't bring out the welcoming squad. I'll check in with you later." She engages her motor and leaves the three of you in her wake.

"I should have asked her to tow us in," Annie says, pulling out some paddles.

An hour later you manage to finish half-sailing, half-paddling your meager ship to Pier Three, which turns out to be a floating dock. It rises and falls gently with the ocean waves. You realize that this is the first time your crew has ever properly docked the *Margit* but, with lots of shouting and scrambling about, they manage. After tying off, you all hop out of the boat.

Annie stands exultantly with her arms stretched out toward the city. Big Billy lays down on the dock and hugs it. You step over him and take a look at the surroundings. There are docks and warehouses near the pier. Farther down the road, you see people walking around. A child rides by on a bicycle.

"I haven't seen one of those in a long time," Annie says.

"The kid or the bike?" Big Billy asks, standing up.

"Both, now that you mention it. Let's check out the town."

The three of you walk around for a while. The yellow roads seem to wind through the port, leading to various restaurants and shops. Black roads crisscross throughout as well, leading to residential buildings. Many of the buildings have a strange architecture that is hard to place. Some seem to spring from the earth, austere and simple at first glance, but subtly audacious and defiant. You notice that many of the buildings have fruit trees growing next to them or in little courtyards out front.

You also notice that, aside from where plants are growing, there seems to be a lot of shade. The locals must not like to tan. Most buildings and businesses have built-in or retractable awnings. Many walkways are partially covered as well, either by strong-looking truss structures or some durable fabric suspended on cables. You appreciate how much more pleasant it is to be out of the sun.

Aside from the architecture, this port city reminds you of any other coastal town. There are palm trees. You see old folks sitting at a café table playing cards. A line of young children follows a man carrying a bag of soccer balls and orange cones. It all looks perfectly normal, but something still doesn't feel quite right about this place. Something has been bothering you ever since you got here. Then you realize what it is. You left the floating dock some time ago, but every once in a while the ground sways gently. You look up at the skyline, and every now and again a building rises and falls ever so slightly.

An older man wearing a bow tie walks by, and you ask him why the buildings are moving.

"Oh, you must be the crew of the *Margit*," he says.

"And the captain asked you a question," Annie says, gesturing at him with her spear.

"Well, okay!" He laughs and puts up his hands. "Let me warn you, though. You should not go around pointing that stick at people. You might get shot."

"Sorry," Annie says, moving the spear behind her back. She keeps a tight grip on it, though.

"The buildings move because they are on water," he says.

Suddenly it all makes sense. "Freeport isn't an island," you say softly, "it's a floating city."

"That is correct," the man says, "and if the tall one would like to stay here, he should stop taking fruit that does not belong to him."

You turn and see Big Billy reaching through a fence to pull peaches from a tree. He freezes when he notices everyone staring. Then he crams the entire peach he is holding into his mouth.

The old man slowly shakes his head. Then he turns back to you and says, "Anyway, yes, this is a floating city. But do not worry, there is not much risk of it sinking. Each section is independent and floats on its own. Even if some of them were to fail, the others would remain above the surface. Though even having one fail is unlikely."

"Why would you build a city on water?" asks Annie.

"It sounds insane, but where else could we escape to? Where else could we build a society that they would not try to control? It was difficult to build Freeport on the sea, but it was impossible to build it anywhere else."

"Who are they?" Annie asks.

"Oh, forgive me for rambling. It is not something you should worry about while you are visiting. Just enjoy your time here. Freeport is capitalism at its finest, so I expect you will."

"I thought this was a libertarian society, not a capitalist one."

"It is both. A capitalist society is one with private property. The more that things are privately owned, the more capitalist a society is. Libertarianism assigns private ownership to all property, so it is naturally a capitalist system. For that reason, libertarian societies tend to be capitalist societies as well."

"So are they the same thing, then?"

"No, not exactly. Capitalism is a subset of libertarianism. You could theoretically have a libertarian society that was not capitalist if, for example, everyone agreed to special property rules. That is the idea behind voluntary communism and systems like that. It would not be communism in the historical sense, where you have some ruling body that forces everyone to participate and tries to direct the economy.

"Anyway, you'll learn all about capitalism as you take in our beautiful city. My advice is: spend time exploring, meet some of the people and, when you get back home, put in a good word for us." The man gives a slight bow and resumes his brisk pace.

"I don't like that guy," Annie says. "He's a weirdo."

You continue walking around and, before too long, you find the market that Chelsea mentioned. There are many things to buy but, given your current situation, you are more interested in selling. Annie takes the lead and negotiates the sale of all of your cargo on the *Margit*. The fresh coconuts are surprisingly valuable; the dried fish less so, as were your handmade tools and textiles, but you manage to sell all of them. Someone even buys Big Billy's portable coconut opener. The most surprising thing, though, is that you get an offer to buy the *Margit*. While not a tremendous amount of money, from talking to merchants around the market, you know it would be enough to buy each of you passage home on one of the trade vessels that come to Freeport. You would even have some left over to spend while you are waiting to leave. Annie says it would be crazy to turn down the offer. You consider the alternative. Sailing home seems unlikely to be easy, or even possible, so you agree. Big Billy does too. Annie sells the *Margit* and gives you and Big Billy appropriate shares of the proceeds.

Now, with a little bit of disposable income and a week until your transport vessel departs, the three of you consider how to spend your time and money. Big Billy thinks for a moment and then heads directly for a shoe store. You don't blame him. Your own feet are so scarred and calloused from walking barefoot on Danger Island that you can hardly remember what it is like to wear shoes.

Annie spots a restaurant and asks if you would like to celebrate with an early dinner. You are hungry, but there is something else you want even more, so you agree to meet back here in three hours. You realize that you really are a tourist now, so you head to the tourist information center that Chelsea mentioned.

The place is full of maps and advertisements. You find a list of hotels, pick a cheap one, and start walking toward it. When you get there, you see a self-service check-in kiosk. It prompts you to purchase a subscription to one of the security companies for the duration of your stay. It comes bundled with some insurance, too. Apparently, you can't stay here without it, but the sign-up process is fast, and the cost is low, so soon you are in your very own no-frills hotel room. Still, after so much time in the wilderness, a simple bed and a hot shower seem like extraordinary luxuries. You take your time in the shower and almost forget where you are.

After washing up, you head back out into the town. The sun has sunk low, and many more people are walking around. You are struck by how normal it seems here. You could be in any city in the world. You see people leaving work and going home to their families or heading to cafés and bars to meet their friends. You pass teenagers who are hanging out after school and being obnoxious. They gawk at you as you walk by and laugh at your clothing. Damn kids.

Then an aroma catches your attention, and you immediately forget the brats. It is coming from across the street. An old woman standing at a food cart mixes something into a frying pan. You walk over and see neat piles of green onions, basil, chili peppers, and limes. She smiles at you expectantly. You pick something from her menu and ask if the price includes tax. She laughs and tells you that taxes are illegal. Then she starts cooking up your order. It smells fantastic.

"So, so. This must be your first time here in Free-port," she says, pronouncing the city's name as two words.

You nod and ask her how long she has been here.

"Oh, only about...one year now. It isn't like my hometown. I am from Chiang Mai. Over 100,000 people there, including my family. I tell them to come here, but they think it is silly to live on a floating island. They think it might sink," she laughs. "My grandchildren will come when they hear how much money I make."

She sprinkles something on top of your food.

"Why did you come here?" she asks.

"It was an accident," you say.

"Very lucky accident. You want to know why I come here?"

"Yes."

"No Thai restaurants! Everywhere else in the world, too much competition. Here, nothing. It's great. My business is a monopoly." She laughs again. "For now anyway. I heard another Thai restaurant is opening soon. It was nice while it lasted."

After a moment, you realize she is joking. A monopoly is generally considered a bad thing in most places around the world. And it is a bad thing when it exists because of a government-granted privilege. The state makes it so that one company can operate a specific business and prevents other companies from competing. That's aggression and, moreover, it is bad for the economy. This Thai restaurant, if you can even call it a restaurant, may have a monopoly by circumstance, but it isn't a problem since anyone is free to open up a competing food cart.

She finishes cooking up your order and gives it to you. You suspect that anything that wasn't coconuts, fish, seaweed, seagull, crab, or clam would have tasted amazing after so long but, after one bite, tears of joy start running down your cheeks. It is so good. Then you realize it isn't the food that is making you so happy it hurts, but the power and support of being part of a community. It is the supply chain of farmers, trucks, boats, and other capital that lets people live on a floating island but still have ingredients from around the world. It is the division of labor and specialization that allows an elderly woman to make a living by chatting with people and cooking on a small street in the middle of the ocean.

"You no like?" the old woman asks.

"It is wonderful, thank you," you tell her, and then step away, so she doesn't see you crying.

A few minutes later, you hear a familiar voice ask, "Did you eat something spicy? Here, have something to drink."

You turn and see Annie smiling at you, wearing a new outfit that looks quite handsome. In one hand she has a bar of dark chocolate, and with the other hand she passes you a cup of some cold, yellow drink. You take it eagerly.

"Someone was thirsty," she says, taking the cup back from you. "We can get more. There's a café around the corner called Freedom Forever. All of their drinks have nerdy names, but I've tried two, and both were outstanding. That was the Carnegie Lemonade."

"It was great, but maybe later. Let's look around a bit."

The two of you start to wander. There are many small stores. You guess that it makes sense to conserve space and weight in a floating city.

After a while you see Chelsea walking by. You wave to her, and she comes over.

"At your service," she says. When she sees the confused look on your face, she explains, "I saw that you're one of my customers now. Well, at least for the next few days."

"And if I ever return, though I wonder how hard it will be to get back out to the middle of the Indian Ocean," you say.

"Freeport isn't stationary. It occasionally moves around the world, albeit slowly. We usually drop anchor near land and stay there for a while, so it should be easier for you to get here next time. Just use a boat built by a professional."

"Very funny. But how will I find you if you are always moving?"

"Well, Freeport rarely changes locations. It's expensive to move this thing around, and it is getting bigger every year. I've even heard rumors that if the city gets too big, they are going to try to split it into two cities. Like cell mitosis."

"Wow."

"Cool, right? The cost isn't the only problem, though. There are not many places where a craft like this can survive for long periods. Fewer and fewer as the city gets larger. Eventually, bad weather comes, and if we are in the wrong place at the wrong time...." She knocks her fists together and then pulls them open and apart.

"You don't seem too worried, though."

"No, I'm not. I've been here for a while, and we've survived every storm. Sometimes there has been damage, but we've also learned a lot. The new linkages are amazing."

"So things weren't always this nice?" you ask.

"Not even close," she says.

"What was it like?" you ask.

Chelsea thinks for a moment and then says, "The first people who lived here were all radicals. Libertarian anarchists. They wanted to build a society based on the non-aggression principle, but they had a hard time finding people who were willing to come. Who cares about liberty if the only things you have to eat are fish and seaweed, right?"

"I can sympathize with that," Annie says.

"Actually, it was worse than that," Chelsea says. "The early sections weren't as stable as these are. Even people who were used to boats would still get motion sickness or have trouble sleeping. People would often slip, trip, or drop something. Accidents happened every day, and every month there was at least one bad one. I mentioned that the food was bad, but fresh water was often in short supply. And sanitation, oh my god. Some people thought they could just dump waste into the ocean. That works fine if you are speeding along under your own power, but if you are stationary or moving slowly, well, the poo floats right along next to you. And it stinks. People were miserable.

"Then came the first real storm, which ripped the sections apart. The connections were strong, but the stresses were enormous. Nowadays, the company models the mechanics of the city as a whole before approving new connections, but back then, they were just excited to grow. Well, they grew too fast. Most sections were recovered, but one sank, and another two stayed connected to each other but were swept away by wind and current. The people on board ended up getting rescued by a military ship, which then used the sections for target practice. Not maliciously; just because the unmanned sections were a hazard and nobody was in a position to collect them. After that, the population dropped by more than half. It took a lot of work before anyone would move in, let alone invest in new sections.

"But eventually, some of the companies based here became successful. They generated enough business that a little economy started. Then the different companies started hiring people. There is nothing like a job to pull someone into your society. Before they knew it, they were surrounded by people who didn't know anything about their libertarian philosophy. These new people just wanted a better life, and Freeport has jobs for everyone. Zero unemployment."

"Zero?"

"Yep. Well, there are people who don't work, but only because they are dependents, or retired, or take care of the kids at home or whatever."

"What about people who can't work, like the sick or disabled?" asks Annie.

"Well, when I said dependents I meant anyone who can't take care of themselves, child or adult. There is no single system for taking care of everyone. With most things in life, there isn't one best solution for everyone. Like you, there are many people who care about others, and they get taken care of. Usually by family; sometimes by strangers. Anyway, my point was that there are no minimum wage laws, so anyone can find a job if they want."

"A job that doesn't pay very much," Annie says.

"True, but some people want those kinds of jobs, and some people don't have the skills for higher-paying jobs. A minimum wage destroys low-paying jobs, but it doesn't create high-paying jobs. If you set a minimum wage, you're not making people richer. You're just taking away opportunities from people who don't have many other options. For some people, those are the only opportunities they have. Take kids, for example."

"Like...child labor?" asks Annie.

"Before your imagination goes wild, what I mean is that there is no minimum age to work in Freeport. It matters more about how mature the person is than their age. I've seen kids as young as twelve get part-time jobs, but I'd say most people who grow up here start working at sixteen. I guess you could hire a five-year-old if you wanted to, but they aren't all that productive, and most parents don't even want to deal with the hassle of their preteens working, let alone someone younger. But if that bothers you, then you are really not going to like some of the other things that are allowed here."

"Like what?" you ask.

"All drugs are legal, even frightening ones like heroin. Except in sections 16 and 17, where the owners banned drugs for personal reasons. But in general, it is legal to buy, sell, or use them."

"Why do they get to change the rules?" you ask.

"They aren't changing the rules, they are just adding additional ones. You are free to eat mussels in Freeport, but you are also free to restrict yourself to vegetarianism if you want."

"And the twelve-year-olds with jobs are free to buy drugs?" you ask.

"There is no arbitrary age limit, but retailers generally won't sell the harder stuff to anyone but adults that they know. They can be liable if they sell drugs to someone who isn't capable of using them responsibly. If they think you are unlikely to keep your drug habit under control, most of them won't sell to you even if you are 30 years old. The same goes for alcohol, weapons, etc. Plus, selling drugs to kids would be a PR nightmare."

"So where do you draw the line?"

"That's the whole point, you don't pick an arbitrary age and expect it to work for everyone. I've seen sixteen-year-olds who are completely conscientious and responsible. I have also seen middle-aged men who I wouldn't trust with a butter knife. There is certainly an age component to being an adult, but age isn't everything. For example, if you sold drugs to someone even though you knew they were going to use it to poison someone else, would you be liable? I spoke with a judge about this, and she said that in some cases you might be. Retailers don't like that risk. So they don't sell to kids or losers who might commit crimes to feed their habit. But I think the main thing is they don't want parents getting upset and causing PR problems for them."

"It sounds like even though these things are legal, people have other reasons for not doing them."

"Yeah. It works out pretty well, and it makes my job a lot easier. It's easier to hold people accountable when the drug production and sales are out in the open. Also, I don't have to worry about a black market smuggling drugs and other things into Freeport. But if that doesn't impress you, then how about this? You can sell parts of your own body if you like. I guess people already sell hair all over the world, but here it's not uncommon to sell blood as well. Doctors buy it for transfusions. People can also sell skin, bone marrow, or even whole organs like kidneys. Some places around the world ban the sale of body parts, so people who need them end up waiting years for donors, but Freeport never has a shortage. Of organs or customers."

"Isn't that dangerous? People might get killed for their organs."

"Unfortunately, that happens regardless. But just like prostitution and drugs, it's easier to keep things safe and honest if the trade is legal and out in the open," Chelsea says.

"Why would people even want to sell their organs in the first place?"

"For the money. I know one man who sold a kidney to pay for a surgery his wife needed. He saved her life. It's not all noble causes, though. Some people just want money to buy things or to gamble away."

You look at yourself and wonder how much your organs are worth.

"You don't seem too put off. Let's see. What will blow your mind? Did you know you can sell babies? Well, in reality, you are selling the right to care for and raise the baby, but it is more fun to say it the first way. It's very similar to the way adoption works in many parts of the world, but the financial component of it bothers people."

"Then people will have kids just to sell them off."

"Yes."

"And you think that is fine?"

"If the child goes to a good home and the parents get a child that they wouldn't have been able to have on their own, why would I have a problem with it? It happens already, but when you normalize it, then it becomes safer for everyone, and fewer kids have to grow up with parents who don't want them."

When you don't respond, Chelsea moves on.

"But these are all pretty minor in the grand scheme of things. It wasn't markets for sex, drugs, or babies that made this place successful."

"What was it, then?"

"It's hard to pick just one thing because there are so many advantages over other cities. No arbitrary trade restrictions. No arbitrary regulations. Lower crime rates."

"Thanks to your vigilance?"

"I don't have much to do with it. Anyone who commits a crime ends up having a hard time living here. Not everyone is a libertarian, but there is a strong culture against aggression, so criminals get ostracized. Not just by people but by businesses, too. Plus, things like rent and insurance get more expensive for high-risk individuals. It's such a hassle that they usually make amends or leave the first chance they get."

"So there is almost no crime?"

"There is still crime, but the rates are relatively low. A lot of my work is in crime prevention, which means walking around and talking to people. Sometimes just standing around at popular bars or big events. When there is a problem, then it's mainly about de-escalating situations, negotiation, and psychology. The company considers it a failure if things get to the point where a security officer like me needs to use violence. That doesn't always work out in practice, though. Everyone who lives here are all just regular people, and people sometimes make bad decisions. There is still domestic abuse, rape, murder. I could tell you some horrible stories." Chelsea looks past you. "The things people do to each other, it makes me sick. This place is supposed to set an example, but crime still happens. We can't even keep our homicide rate at zero. It makes me wonder if there is no hope for humanity."

Chelsea looks back at you and forces a smile.

"Don't get me wrong; if there were any place you would want to be a cop, this would be it. And, truth be told, things are getting better here. I guess I have higher expectations for us than the rest of the world. We did a study of crimes in Freeport over the last few years that showed a correlation between crime and how long someone had lived here. You probably won't be surprised to hear that the most recent people to arrive were also the most likely to commit crimes. It makes me hopeful that eventually the kids who are growing up here will be much more peaceful and respectful than their parents' generation. And maybe their kids won't even have to hear rumors about violent crimes, at least not within their own community.

"Anyway, as you can imagine, most of my job is keeping an eye on children and visitors like you. No offense."

"None taken," you say.

"I don't think we're the ones you need to worry about," Annie says.

Chelsea waits patiently to hear more, but Annie keeps her mouth shut.

"Where is your other friend, by the way? I haven't had a chance to catch up with him."

"We haven't seen him," you say.

"Okay, well I'm going to get back to work. Enjoy the rest of your evening," Chelsea says.

After Chelsea leaves, the two of you stop at a bench to sit and watch people walk past. You ask Annie for another sip of her drink, hand it back to her, and then continue digging into your food.

"This place is nice," she says. "I'd forgotten how wonderful it is to be around so many people. Did you know they have two theaters? Two! I'm almost tempted to stay for more than a week, especially after talking to my agent. He's got nothing lined up for me.

You swallow hard and then laugh. "Your agent? You spoke with him? He probably thought you were dead."

"He did. My family even had a funeral for me. Crazy, right?"

"Wow," is all you say. You had forgotten how long it has been. You wonder what you have missed while you have been away.

"Anyway, we'll all be back soon, so it doesn't matter. What are you doing later? We should check out the rest of the city."

"Sounds like you have been enjoying yourself," you say.

"Yes," she says, "and I'm looking forward to even more fun tonight. But first, let's get you out of those clothes and into something more comfortable." She takes you by the hand and leads you toward some shops.

Stefan Molyneux

"First and foremost, although I am an anarchist, I am not a utopian. There is no social system which will utterly eliminate evil. In a stateless society, there will still be rape, theft, murder and abuse. To be fair, just and reasonable, we must compare a stateless society not to some standard of otherworldly perfection, but rather to the world as it already is. The moral argument for a stateless society includes the reality that it will eliminate a large amount of institutionalized violence and abuse, not that it will result in a perfectly peaceful world, which of course is impossible. Anarchy can be viewed as a cure for cancer and heart disease, not a prescription for endlessly perfect health. It would be unreasonable to oppose a cure for cancer because such a cure did not eliminate all other possible diseases–in the same way, we cannot reasonably oppose a stateless society because some people are bad, and a free society will not make them good."

ANARCHY

The next day, you decide to explore the city. You feel great walking around in your new outfit, and it is immediately apparent that you are drawing less attention than yesterday. It makes it much easier to get around and mingle.

You reach the outskirts of the city and look out. The view is breathtaking. After a few minutes, someone walks up next to you.

"My office has a nice view, right?" Chelsea says.

"You're not following me, are you?" you ask.

"No. Freeport isn't that big yet, so we'll probably cross paths every day. I can leave if you want to be alone," Chelsea says.

"That's okay. I don't know many people here, so it would be nice to chat a little."

"Have you spotted anything out there? Sometimes I look for turtles when I am taking a break. There were little turtles where I grew up, but out here they are gigantic. It's one of the benefits of living out here. The ocean is full of interesting creatures."

"Is that why you moved here?" you ask.

"To Freeport? No. I was looking for work and saw a job posting online that looked unusually lucrative. Back then, they were paying more for female applicants but, nowadays, there are almost as many women here as men. Anyway, they said they would pay for my travel expenses, so I told my parents to kiss my ass and moved out."

"Just like that?"

"Yeah, they were shocked, then stressed, but eventually they got over it."

"What were they worried about? Freeport seems like a nice place to live."

"It is now, but it was different back then. Three things bothered them. First, the population was over 90% male when I moved. That made them worry about my safety. Second, it's a floating city, which at first glance seems dangerous, and, I admit, it is dangerous to some extent. Third, the idea of anarchy is terrifying to most people."

"Anarchy?" you ask.

Chelsea nods her head. "Nobody told you? There's no government here."

"No."

"Oh. Surprise!" Chelsea smiles. "It's not as scary as it sounds. I guess I should give you the basics. Let's see. Anarchy is the absence of government. You may have heard that anarchy means chaos, but life here is basically the same as everywhere else. The only difference is that private companies provide police services, court services, etc. You have to pay the police directly, but you don't pay taxes, so you end up a little ahead. I guess it's kind of boring now that I think about it."

"What about people who can't afford to pay?"

"Basic services are pretty cheap; less than a mobile phone bill. I haven't heard of anyone who couldn't afford them. That said, most people get some coverage from their employer or landlord. We also have a free service tier."

"Free?"

"Yeah. It's valuable for us to have people in the system, so anyone who signs up gets some limited service and priority for pro bono work."

"If there is no government, then are the different security companies you mentioned the only police?"

"Yes, and there are three of them. But one is sort of niche and mainly works with businesses."

"So, if someone isn't your customer then you don't help them?"

"What? No. If there is an emergency any cop would help regardless of who is in trouble. We have agreements with the other companies for handling situations with their customers. But even if someone does not subscribe to any police agency, we still do pro bono work in an emergency or for anyone who can't afford it."

"Why?"

"It's good PR. People prefer to be members if you're the kind of police who help those in need. Some people even donate money to help fund general security or for special projects. Of course, some people just want the lowest price, which is fine, too. I probably shouldn't talk up my competition, but all of the police around here are decent people. You sort of have to be to last in this business. Too many bad reviews, and you get fired."

"If you help anyone, then why would anyone subscribe in the first place?"

"Well, cops usually aren't around when a crime happens, so most of the work happens before and after the fact. Members get priority when it comes to security cameras, patrols, and casework. And we price things so that it's a lot cheaper to be a member than to try to sign up after you have a problem. Also, a lot of our job is getting to know people and neighborhoods because that makes us more effective at solving problems. That creates a lot of value for our customers, so members get much more benefit than non-members who are just hoping one of us is nearby when something bad happens."

"Still, some people choose not to sign up at all. Some want to handle their own security. Others just don't want to be in our system for privacy reasons. Everyone has to decide for themselves, but, given how cheap a membership is, I think it's worth it. Take me for example. I'm a cop, and even I have a subscription. And it's to a competing company!"

"Okay, but what about things that people have to use, like roads? Who is in charge of common resources?"

"Everything is privately owned, even places open to the public like streets and parks."

"I get that, but how does it work?"

"Oh, well some roads are owned by businesses. Section owners usually build roads on their modules for better connection deals. I don't own a section yet, so I don't know all the details. Every module connected to Freeport has some sort of walkway on it. Modules that have businesses provide public roads just to get foot traffic. Foot traffic is considered very valuable, so businesses and module owners pay a premium to be near other high traffic modules. The value of your section will be higher, and you can usually get a better location in Freeport, if you have public roads. The same goes for public space like parks.

"There are a few companies that build and maintain them. Let me tell you, I talk to people on the streets all day, and the road business isn't an easy job here. One road guy likes to talk my ear off. He goes on and on about how the roads need to have excellent drainage and the materials need to be lightweight and resistant to the salt, sun, and stress as the sections flex."

"Sounds tough."

"Yeah, much easier on land. But if you think roads are tough, imagine the work that goes into the sections. The early versions are all gone now, and not for lack of trying. The ocean is just that harsh of an environment. You should see the maintenance they do on the sections when we drop anchor. You can watch companies lift them entirely out of the water. It's crazy.

"As for parks and the like, I know that Thoreau Park is usually free for day-to-day use, but they sometimes charge money for larger events like weddings. The landscaper told me that the parks get most of their money from other section owners who pay for guaranteed relative positioning of their sections."

"But if there's no government, who is making all of these rules about where people can live? Who makes the laws?" you ask.

"Everything is done by private companies. The connection agreements are between the section owners, including the company that owns the core sections. Sections are very expensive, so usually the connection agreements are in place long before they are built.

"Laws are also made by private companies. Unlike other places, laws here don't have arbitrary power. Instead, they simply try to explain the implications of the NAP in different scenarios and society as it presently exists. Causing conflict is the only thing that is against the law, so in one sense, it is pretty simple. But, having a single generic law isn't that useful when you're on the beat. So we buy rules, guidelines, case studies, and other helpful materials that these companies create. Sometimes it is obvious when something goes wrong and who the bad guy is, but other times I don't know if someone is just being an asshole or if they crossed the line and broke the law. So I use their reference materials or call them and ask for help.

"One thing that makes policing easier here is that there are no victimless crimes. When you have a government, sometimes they make things illegal even if they don't hurt anyone, like recreational drug use. We don't have to waste time trying to control how people spend their free time. It makes my job easier, but the idea bothers some people. It's one of the things that worried my mother the most.

"My parents found out that prostitution is perfectly legal, even respectable, here, and my mother immediately assumed that I had chosen that particular profession. So she called me and started going on and on about how I needed to come home and settle down and do something decent with my life.

"I was so mad. First, because I wanted to tell her off for just assuming what I was doing without even bothering to ask me. She's always been like that. More importantly, I was annoyed because it is attitudes like hers that make prostitution such a dangerous job where I come from. In places like Freeport, it is totally safe. But I was in a bad mood, so instead of explaining all this to her or telling her what I was really going to be doing for a living, I just told her there's nothing wrong with being a prostitute and that she shouldn't knock it until she tries it."

Chelsea laughs and goes on.

"Well, that made her really upset. I felt bad, so, later on, I told my father the truth. He was relieved and more than happy to break the news to my mom. My mother didn't talk to me for a while, but eventually she got over it. They never got over the idea of anarchy, though. I tried to explain that life isn't that different. That there are police and that I was even going to be part of the police. But in their heads, they were picturing some violent pit where people live like wild beasts.

"It took a long time before they would come to visit. My father doesn't like boats, so that was his excuse. Now that I think about it, that seems like such a long time ago. Things have changed."

"How so?"

"I'd say almost everything has improved. It used to be a little awkward when there were fewer people and it felt like everyone knew everybody else. It makes dating hard. It makes drama with friends more annoying. Once we grew beyond two or three thousand people, things felt more normal. There are now many people my age who I have never met. And enough people are moving in and out that it keeps things interesting."

"Fascinating."

"Well, I need to get back to my beat. Someone reported a missing marine VHF radio, and I am on the case. See you around."

You watch her leave and wonder if this is really what anarchy looks like. People are going about their lives, working, having families, going out at night. It seems like there isn't much difference between a libertarian society and many other parts of the world. But there is a difference. You could feel it as you walked around. These people aren't afraid of the police. They aren't worried about being put in jail for doing drugs or starting a business. The rules are simple: Follow the non-aggression principle, and then do as you please. Each one of them is in charge of their own life and can live it with confidence. It's a flourishing of the human spirit, and most of them don't even notice or care. They have an abundance of liberty and capital, but this is just normal life to them. You guess that being stranded for so long makes you appreciate these things. For you, it is exhilarating just to be around buildings and have reliable access to fresh water. Life for these people is grand.

Then you wonder if it could be life for you as well. Would you give up everything you have at home, your old life, for a chance at even greater freedom? They have internet access, food delivery, and many of the other comforts of modern life. Could you find a job and make new friends here? You think about it as you walk around.

As it gets closer to lunchtime, there is a lot more foot traffic. You stop at a café offering cheap food and order some grilled fish. It is simple but tasty, with a little salt and lemon. As you eat, the old man from the other day walks in and orders the same thing.

"You have good taste," you say, nodding toward the fish on your plate.

"You have good financial sense," he replies, sitting down next to you. "My name is Dirk, by the way. Where is your bodyguard?"

"Probably still sleeping." You remember having a lot of fun with Annie last night.

"And what brings you to Freeport, captain?"

"Actually, I sold my ship, so I'm not a captain anymore. Now that I think about it, I'm not much of anything at the moment, except maybe a tourist. We are just hanging out for a few days until we can make our way home."

"It is not a bad place to be a tourist. Tourists are consumers, and, in an anarcho-capitalist society like Freeport, the consumer is king."

"What is anarcho-capitalism? Is that what you do here? You said before that this place is capitalist, but Chelsea said it is anarchist."

"Anarcho-capitalism is just pure, unadulterated capitalism. It is pure in a few respects. The first is that it does not allow exceptions to the NAP. Back in the day, most libertarians believed that there was no way for the free market to provide certain services like police and courts. So they decided that the non-aggression principle had to have a few exceptions. Anarcho-capitalism was the name adopted by libertarians who rejected the idea that there should be exceptions to the NAP. These "ancaps" said that aggression could never be justified and that we should never legitimize it. Most societies around the world practice capitalism out of necessity, but all of them deviate from the non-aggression principle to some extent. Anarcho-capitalism is the extreme: all capitalism and no aggression. People usually see a connection between capitalism and libertarianism, but most still do not understand exactly how they are related."

"So ancaps are the hardcore libertarians?"

"Yes, but nowadays people know that anarchy is the logical conclusion of libertarianism, so we do not need to distinguish between them as much. So I like to tell people that I am a libertarian. It is a little easier to say. But anarcho-capitalism is pure in another sense as well. With pure capitalism, you determine ownership by the private property system, and that is it.

"Other social systems have special rules for distributing property differently, usually to redistribute property from those who would own it under a capitalist system to special groups of other people. For example, under absolute monarchy, the monarch owns everything. In less extreme systems, the government might partially follow the private property system but then force people to hand over part of their income each year.

"Anarcho-capitalism rejects any such deviations from the private property system. So when I say anarcho-capitalism is pure, I mean this in the sense that it does not have special voluntary or involuntary arrangements for property."

"So ancaps are the hardcore capitalists?"

"Yes, but there is a third way to think about anarcho-capitalism, that it adopts the purest form of anarchy. Some anarchists still believe that in addition to having no government, anarchists should be against companies, working for wages, or even just working in general. Anarcho-capitalism, on the other hand, is just anarchy in the sense that there are no rulers. Voluntary relationships are just fine, even if they are hierarchies like families and businesses.

"When it comes to aggression, however, it does not matter if you are a lone thief or a giant government extorting taxes. Anarcho-capitalism does not allow it. So ancaps are anarchists, plain and simple. Other types of anarchism tend to dilute the core message with other values."

"So ancaps are the hardcore anarchists?"

"Yes. It might seem silly to make all of these distinctions, but ideas are important. Why have another name for capitalism? It emphasizes the fact that you cannot have pure capitalism if your society has a government. So if you are talking to someone who thinks a society with a limited government practices capitalism, then you can use the term anarcho-capitalism to distinguish a society that is one-hundred percent capitalist. Likewise, the name is useful to distinguish one-hundred percent libertarianism from mixed systems that compromise the core values to some extent.

"For example, minarchism tries to increase liberty by having a government that is as small as possible, typically only police, courts, and a military. That would be a great improvement in most places, and many libertarians are minarchists. But they could be a little more libertarian if they realized that libertarian anarchy is possible, and stopped supporting government entirely."

"So it seems like you are saying that libertarianism, capitalism, and anarchy all go together?"

Dirk takes a few bites of food and thinks about how to respond.

"Not quite. An anarcho-capitalist society is capitalist, libertarian, and anarchist all at the same time, but these three systems do not have to go together. A libertarian society must be an anarchist society, but an anarchist society need not be libertarian. Let me explain. A libertarian society must be an anarchist society because government necessarily violates the non-aggression principle. Any government you have, no matter how small, would compromise the core value of libertarianism. But you can still have crime without government, so an anarchist society need not be libertarian. Animals live in this kind of anarchy, and some men aspire to it. They wish to be totally unconstrained and have their way with the world. A fine thing when you are the strongest, but someone stronger always comes along.

"Similarly, a capitalist society must be libertarian but a libertarian society need not be capitalist. A capitalist society has to be libertarian because any deviation from libertarianism would change the ownership of property away from the capitalist ideal. But, as I mentioned, you could have a libertarian society that is not capitalist. Such as a group of monks who live together in caves and make cheese. They might live perfectly libertarian lives, but have a head monk who decides what work everyone does and what property each person gets. That is not capitalism, but it very well could be libertarian.

"Sorry if this is too much detail. I was not sure how technical you wanted to get, but the upshot is that capitalism is a type of libertarianism, which is a type of anarchism.

"Some people find this confusing, but that is okay. The trouble is the confusion about what government is. Some see it as the solution to all of life's problems, but, in reality, it is just organized aggression that has gained legitimacy. Government is any organization that society exempts from the non-aggression principle. It is held to a lower ethical standard than everyone else. You cannot tell people what they can and cannot eat, but if the government does it, magically it becomes okay.

"People try to justify the double standard by saying that the ends justify the means. It is true that sometimes government will do something you like, but sometimes it will do something you do not like. However, every time government does anything at all, it aggresses against somebody. That person is forced to participate in something that they do not agree with. Strip away all the veneer and what do you get? No matter how good the intentions, the method is always aggression.

"That is why, from a libertarian perspective, governments should not exist. It is for the same reason theft and murder should not exist. If you think that crime is bad, then to be consistent you need to say that government is bad as well. It is the same problem on a different scale. One is bottom-up, and the other is top-down. At the end of the day, you are left with the same conclusion: The world should be free of conflict. No muggers and no tax collectors. No murderers and no wars."

"That seems like an impossible dream."

"Getting rid of all crime is utopian. Children seem hard-wired to steal things, and even some adults in Freeport intentionally commit crimes. And while getting rid of governments might be next-to-impossible in the short term, in the long term I think it is merely difficult. States are only semi-stable institutions. Since they are parasitic, there will always be tension between the rulers and the slaves. Most governments have done a good job of indoctrinating their subjects into supporting them, and people do. So much so that many people love their servitude. If their masters disappeared overnight, they would beg someone to step in and take hold of their chains."

"Then why are you so optimistic?"

"Two reasons. First, lies take much more effort to maintain than the truth, and the idea that government is a necessary evil is a lie. Government is evil, period. We get along just fine without it here in Freeport, and I am hopeful other parts of the world will start to join us.

"Second, you can always count on self-interest. As technology makes government more and more irrelevant, people will naturally tend to want to cast it off. Governments try to maintain monopolies on certain industries to justify their existence, but private companies always find a way around them. There have been taxi, postal, telecommunication, and electricity monopolies. All created by government and dying due to innovation. There are more private security guards in the world than government police. There are more private court cases than public ones. There are still other monopolies that need to go, like money production, but even there, cracks are starting to form. Eventually, private companies will provide everything people want. People will choose the free-market solutions simply because they are better. Then governments will wither away, and we will be able to keep them from rising again."

"Everything is black and white, then? Good versus evil?" you ask. Dirk closes his eyes and shakes his head.

"The principles are black and white, but reality is a big, colorful mess. Some people think good is the opposite of evil, but that is not true. Other people think that they can accomplish good through evil, which is not only false, but repulsive. I have met politicians who have good intentions and are generally trying to make the best of a bad situation. But the individual politicians are not the problem—it is the system that produces so much evil.

"Material things are not evil. Not guns, nor money, nor drugs. The only thing that can be evil is purposeful behavior. Only causing conflict is evil. Everything else is necessarily not-evil. But even if I can get them to understand the concept at a theoretical level, they continue taxing, regulating, and so on.

"Unethical behavior is evil, and ethical behavior is not. But ethical behavior is not necessarily good, either. People do bad things to themselves all the time, but as long as it does not interfere with the lives of others, then that is their prerogative. Good is the opposite of bad, but good and bad are subjective and apply to anything, not just action."

"If good is subjective, why can't you accomplish good through evil?"

"Well, I guess technically you can. A thief thinks it is good for him to have your money. But with evil actions, you guarantee bad results for someone. There is always a victim. With non-evil actions, there is a chance that nobody loses out, and there is also a chance that many people benefit. I think people tend to overstate the good and overlook the bad when they think about what their evil plans will accomplish."

"Are you some kind of philosopher?"

"No, just a businessman who likes to read."

"What kind of business are you in?"

"I am an engineer, or at least I was in my younger days. Nowadays, I guess you might call me an entrepreneur. Regardless of the role, I have always been doing the same thing."

"What's that?"

"Increasing freedom for my customers."

"Because you love capitalism?"

"Because that is what all businesses do, whether they make products or provide services. Whatever they offer, it helps people do what they want to do, or even things they did not even know they could do."

"Do you prefer the technology side or the business side better?"

"I enjoyed my life working as an engineer, but I wonder if that is just because I was young and strong. Then again, when I look at my schedule, and it is all meetings and conference calls, I am not so sure. Speaking of which, I need to be going. Enjoy your stay, keep an eye out for land, and at some point treat yourself to the ceviche they serve here."

"I will," you say, unsure of which point you are agreeing to.

Dirk nods and stands up to leave. As he goes, he waves to the woman behind the counter, and she says, "See you next week."

On Danger Island, you were were focused on solving the occasional conflicts that arose between you, Annie, and Big Billy. So, you never considered applying libertarian ethics to organizations, especially the governments back in modern society. It hadn't occurred to you that you were living in a state of anarchy. It was simple and small scale, but it was implicit in how you all worked together. Now, Dirk has laid it out explicitly, and it is hard to see how the non-aggression principle could lead to any other conclusion. Maybe it would have been obvious if you had grown up here.

You sit for a while, watching people walk by. As you finish your meal, you start to imagine how they all got here. Were they trying to escape persecution or just looking for work? How many of these kids were born here? You walk out of the café and wonder what it is like to grow up in a place like this. When the native children go out into the world, will they look back and see a birdcage or an oasis?

You see your reflection in a window and think to yourself, "Who would I be if I had been shaped and educated in a place that values life, liberty, and property?"

Lew Rockwell

"It isn't a coincidence that governments everywhere want to educate children. Government education, in turn, is supposed to be evidence of the state's goodness and its concern for our well-being. The real explanation is less flattering. If the government's propaganda can take root as children grow up, those kids will be no threat to the state apparatus. They'll fasten the chains to their own ankles. H.L. Mencken once said that the state doesn't just want to make you obey. It tries to make you want to obey. And that's one thing the government schools do very well."

Purposeful Behavior

The question of what growing up here would have been like is still fresh in your mind when a troop of young children in swimsuits marches past you. They head to a nearby pool where other children are swimming. You guess that swimming is one of the first things they teach you when you grow up on the ocean. That makes sense, but why bother building a pool with so much ocean all around? Then again, you are dealing with people who decided to construct a city on water.

You lean against a fence while watching two children fight over an inflatable shark and wonder if sharks make it too dangerous for kids to swim in the open ocean. Then you see a swimming instructor calling those children out of the pool and wonder how children fit in with the non-aggression principle.

You know the NAP does not make exceptions for any particular class of people, be they young, old, male, female, etc. But children seem to be systematically treated differently all over the world. Is that ethically justified? One adult should not force another adult to eat something, even if it is good for them. But parents make their children eat vegetables when the children do not want to. Do conflicts arise between children and their parents? If they do, who is responsible for these conflicts?

Children and their parents often disagree about what the child should do. The child wants to eat candy, but the parent thinks the child should eat healthy food. The child wants to play with knives, but the parent takes them away. But, again, you know that the same is sometimes valid for adults. An adult who unwittingly tries to eat a poisonous fruit, like a child who finds cleaning chemicals, might have it ripped from their hands by someone who knows better. An adult who is delirious from illness might get spoon-fed and bathed like a baby or restrained for their own safety. Similarly, just as helping an adult might at first seem like conflict, the way adults typically interact with children might incorrectly appear to be aggression.

By comparing a child to an impaired adult, it seems that children are not a special case ethically. The difference in how people treat them is merely due to their physiological and psychological differences. These differences affect the analysis of the NAP, but not because they are children. When those same mental and physical differences occur in adults, those adults can be treated like children as well. When someone becomes old or ill, they too are taken care of like children. But even for the elderly, age is not a determining factor. If someone is old but mentally and physically capable, they will be treated like an adult. Similarly, if a ten-year-old is as mentally and physically capable as an adult, then from an ethical perspective, they should be treated like an adult as well.

Of course, the reality is that children are typically different from the average adult both mentally and physically. What does this imply about how adults can treat them from an ethical perspective?

A woman walks up next to you and breaks your train of thought.

"Which one is yours?" she asks, nodding to the squealing horde in the pool.

"Oh, none. I was just walking by," you say.

"Mine is the fat one with the mohawk. He thinks he is good at swimming, but I think he is just buoyant."

Her son's haircut makes it easy for you to pick him out of the crowd.

"If you are looking for a school, this is one of the best. They put a lot of effort into tailoring the program to the students. I remember hating school, but the way they run this operation makes me wish I was a kid again. I went to public school when I was little, and I still occasionally have bad dreams about it. You know, nightmares about being late to class or being bullied by other kids. It's like I have some sort of mild PTSD.

"Because of that, I always thought that when I had kids, I would homeschool them. But after we moved here, it didn't seem to make sense. Prices are reasonable, and the schools here don't have the problems that the government schools did, so why not use them? And I think that it's even more important when he gets older and starts learning advanced topics. I'm not sure I could teach him those even if I wanted to. I'm planning to use online classes at that point, but who knows. I'll figure it out in a few years.

"I think the schools are better here because back on land, they try to have one school system for everyone. In Freeport, anyone can start any kind of school of any size. Some parents just want babysitting, and some want their kids to learn specific topics. There is a pretty wide variety of options here. It's so much easier to just pick what you want, rather than having a single system for everyone and fighting over what it should be."

The noise in the pool gets louder, and the two of you look over at the commotion. The children are playing tag. One of the children gets taken out of the pool for misbehaving.

"The adults are very patient with the kids," you say. "I haven't seen them spank a single child. They just talk to them."

"It's funny you should say that. Before we moved here, my husband and I knew a couple who honestly thought that physical beatings are the best way to teach children. Their parents beat them, so they beat their children. For some kids, it seems to work, but I have never heard a convincing argument about why it is the best way, let alone even justified. Personally, I would never hit a child. I wouldn't even leave someone alone with my child—any child for that matter—who would use violence to shape my child's behavior. That's abusive. I'm a big believer in peaceful parenting. If you want to live in a world where people don't use aggression to solve their problems, you have to raise children without using aggression. If it doesn't seem like a normal part of the world when they are young, I think they won't be as likely to rationalize it as adults.

"Though honestly, this isn't some ideological experiment. I want to raise my son the best I can, so this is mainly for his benefit. If he has no inclination toward aggression, then he'll naturally find better solutions to problems and be a more effective and productive person. And have more friends. That's what the brochure said, anyway. Ask me again in twenty years."

You don't remember asking in the first place, but you consider what she said. Barring conflict, it would be aggression to hit an adult to try to improve their behavior. So there is no reason to think hitting kids would be any different. Furthermore, children are more vulnerable than adults, so from an ethical perspective, you probably need to be more careful with them both physically and mentally. Physical abuse of a child is more damaging and can have long-term adverse effects. The bodily injury might be the same, but it magnifies the aggression. Not to mention that physical interactions that may be fine for adults, like roughhousing, might be aggression when done with children.

Similarly, children are more vulnerable mentally. Things that one might be able to say to an adult without causing conflict could be aggression with children. So adults need to take extra care not to violate the NAP when dealing with children or other vulnerable people. Exposing an adult to violent or sexual imagery might not bother them at all. Exposing a child to the same could cause incredible stress and have long-term repercussions on their health and development.

This lady doesn't seem like the type to harm her child, either physically or mentally. However, you could definitely see her controlling what her son can eat. Left to his own devices, her son might eat cupcakes for every meal. It would typically be aggression to stop an adult from doing that, so why do parents get to do it with their kids? You wonder if one reason might be that kids do not always understand the consequences of their actions. So just as you might forcefully stop an adult from unwittingly eating something poisonous, ensuring that a child eats a healthy diet might not be aggression. Perhaps other controls that parents put on the lives of their children are similarly justified. But you know that there are parents who take things too far and exert so much control that it inhibits their child's development. That would be aggression, so parents are in a difficult position of trying to provide just the right amount of support. You ask the young mother what she thinks about being a parent.

"It's a tough job, but it's rewarding. When my son was about a month old, my husband asked, 'What were we thinking?' It was so much work. But it's getting easier. I can see why some people don't want to have children, though. It's a lot of responsibility."

You wonder about that responsibility, though. Typically, libertarianism does not obligate someone to do anything. It only requires you to avoid taking actions that cause conflict. So why should parents need to take responsibility for their child at all? Just being a biological parent does not seem to create any special relationship from an ethical perspective. Ethics is about action. A person could have their genetic material stolen and end up with a biological child that they never meet or even know exists. How could a conflict be your fault just because your DNA was used to create someone else? If someone cloned you, there is no basis within the libertarian ethical system for establishing an obligation. You can't think of a way in which having matching DNA would necessarily lead to conflict.

What about adoptive parents? It's hard to think about in the context of an established society where you need to factor in social norms, let alone one you are unfamiliar with like Freeport. So, your imagination returns to Danger Island. If you were there and found a child alone in the wilderness, what would the non-aggression principle have to say about how you could interact with it? Assuming the child is mentally mature enough, it would engage in purposeful behavior, and the NAP would apply to it. So, regardless of whether you decide to take care of it, it is an actor, and its property rights must be respected. You would not be able to hurt the child or cause some other conflict with it, but the NAP would not obligate you to care for it, either. You might feel some emotional drive or some moral duty to do so, but there would be no ethical obligation. It does not matter that you are nearby and might be its only chance for survival.

You are going to behave ethically, but you still have the choice of whether to do something good or something bad according to your moral framework. Most people think it is good to try to take care of children, and most moral systems around the world say that it is good to help people. But ethics does not say what is good or what is bad, only how to resolve conflict. Your particular ethical system only prohibits you from causing conflict.

If you choose to take care of the child for a few days or even a few years and then change your mind, that would still be ethical. Of course, many would consider it immoral. You might provide substandard care, like only giving the child half of what it needs to be healthy or provide it water but no food. Not great, but better than nothing, and there is no reason to think that doing so would violate the NAP under normal circumstances. Therefore, acting as a caretaker does not create any exceptions to the non-aggression principle. No one may commit aggression, but no one takes on any obligations either.

You might create obligations if the child is old enough and you make a deal with them, but that is just like making a contract with an adult who needs care. Similarly, if you made a deal with someone else in which you agreed to take care of the child, that would create an obligation. So your actions might make you responsible for a child's welfare, but they don't seem to have much to do with biological reproduction.

When people have children, they usually make them, then take care of them, then watch as they go off into the world on their own. Is there anything in that process that creates an obligation? Something that parents do that would require them to care for a child?

One thing that parents do is exclude other adults from raising their children. There is nothing unethical about this—people exclude others from all sorts of things that they might want all the time. Every time you harvested a coconut on Danger Island, you prevented Annie and Big Billy from picking and eating it. What would have been unethical is if you had tried to prohibit those two from using things that nobody else was using. It would not cause conflict for them to harvest a coconut you were not using and had no intention of using yourself. If you tried to stop them from harvesting any coconuts at all, then you would be causing a conflict.

A closer example to childcare is trade. If Big Billy wants to sell a fish and you want to buy it, then you can exclude Annie from buying it. But you can only do so by actually trading with Big Billy and taking advantage of his offer before Annie does. If you tried to stop her from trading by getting in the way, then you would be causing conflict. The conflict would not just be with Annie, though. You would be preventing Big Billy from trading as well.

The same is true for taking care of a child. If you find a child in the wilderness, it is ethical not to take care of it. If you decide to take care of it, it is ethical to exclude Annie. But if you choose not to take care of it, then it is unethical to stop Annie from taking care of the child. She should be allowed to look after the child if you are not going to.

When it was just you and the child that you were considering, it would have been ethical to provide or withdraw care whenever you wanted. Now that Annie is in the picture, things are a little different. You can exclude Annie, but only if you are going to take care of the child. If you tell Annie that you are going to be the child's caretaker, but then you do not take care of the child, you will have violated the NAP. You will have unethically excluded Annie, but you will also have prevented the child from being in a relationship that it would have wanted. You would be causing conflict with both of them, just as if you had prevented Annie from trading with Big Billy.

Again, the age of the people involved is not important per se. A similar situation could occur between three adults. Back on the island when Big Billy passed out drunk on the shore, he was as helpless as a child. You and Annie had no obligation to help him, but you decided to anyway. But what if Annie had convinced you that she would save Big Billy and it would be better for you to spend time inspecting the ship that you had just pulled from the sand? She would have gotten herself into an ethical bind. If she deliberately let Big Billy drown, she would have caused him to die when he otherwise would have lived. It would have been murder. If you had not been around or had not wanted to help Big Billy, then it would have been tragic, but not unethical, for Annie to let him drown.

In isolation, abandoning a child does not violate the NAP. But it could in the context of certain societies, including most modern societies. The way that human action intertwines can create ethical obligations. You have seen this with contracts and social norms, and a similar effect is possible with caretaking, whether the person being taken care of is a child or an adult. Of course, having an obligation to protect the child's welfare does not mean that the caretaker must personally provide the care. They could hire someone else to do it or find someone else to take on the responsibility and adopt the child. Still, in certain contexts, failure to provide care somehow would be a crime called neglect.

So adopting a child is very different from being a biological parent and much more important from an ethical perspective. In the context of a larger society, the child's new caretaker is choosing to take on the responsibility of ensuring a healthy childhood, either by raising the child or finding someone else who will.

What about the obligations of children to their caretakers? Does the child have corresponding obligations? Certainly not to the biological parents, for the same reasons a person doesn't have automatic obligations to their biological children. What about to a temporary caretaker? A temporary caretaker can withdraw caretaking services whenever they want, so there is no reason to think the child would have any obligations either. What about to an adopted parent who is ethically obligated to ensure the child's wellness? Even here, the parent took on the obligation unilaterally, so there is no reason to think that a child, let alone a baby, would have some obligation in return.

One thing that seems tricky about acting as a caretaker is that what is or is not aggression changes over time. You may need to do things for children when they are young, but as they grow older those same activities can become unethical. You must continually re-evaluate what interactions are appropriate as a child matures and only do what is appropriate at the individual child's stage of development.

For example, before the child can safely walk around, you might keep it in a bassinet for its protection. Once it can get around on its own, you cannot force it to stay in the bassinet anymore. Doing so is no longer promoting the child's development, but inhibiting it. A child who only ever hears baby talk might never learn to use language correctly. The care that is necessary for younger children could retard the development of an older child. In the same way, what might be beneficial for older children could be abusive to a younger child.

In either case, overzealous or overprotective care could cause conflict and therefore be abuse. Libertarianism requires caretaking efforts to fall somewhere in the wide gap between neglect and abuse. If all goes well, then the caretaking ends with the child becoming an adult.

From an ethical perspective, a child becomes an adult when there is nothing left that a caretaker must do in their stead. This transformation happens gradually over time in many different ways. It is not an arbitrary age or a declaration of independence. It is a state of being. It is when they are truly able to stand on their own as an individual. From the caretaker's point of view, this is when they are free of any obligations that they may have taken on. It is also when there are no longer any aspects of the young adult's life that the caretaker can ethically control.

Your neighbor muses while watching the kids play. "Child development is so interesting. I'm a biologist by background, but I've been reading up on psychology and how the brain works. Sometimes these kids are like wild animals, and sometimes they are like little adults. Sometimes you can tell by the look on their faces that there is an internal struggle going on. Different parts of their brains fighting for different outcomes."

You nod idly.

"I love watching them run around, but I can't stay too much longer. Need to go walk my dog soon," the woman says.

Dog. You have been thinking about kids so much, but you forgot about animals. How does the NAP apply to them? You killed and ate more than a few animals while you were on Danger Island to stay alive. At the time, you felt like the NAP only applied to humans, but were you merely rationalizing your behavior? And what about plants? You killed some of those, too, for both food and shelter. Not to mention all the trees you cut down to fix up the *Margit*. If you want to follow the non-aggression principle, do you need to apply it to all living things? Viruses? Rocks?

It seems strange to apply a rule for helping humans get along to things that are not humans. Then again, if humans ever meet intelligent extraterrestrials, why should their purposeful behavior be an exception to the non-aggression principle? Just because they look different? And if there is at least one case where non-humans would fall under the NAP, it makes sense to consider where else the NAP should be applied.

The idea of purposeful behavior is the basis of the non-aggression principle. You know that rocks and other inanimate objects do not have intentions but merely react to the physical laws of the universe like gravity. Praxeology only cares about action, so libertarianism does not concern itself with the way humans interact with non-actors. You can smash stones all day as long as nobody else owns them. The same goes for simple tools and machines.

Some living things are similarly mechanistic. Single-celled organisms, mushrooms, plants, and many animals show complex behavior but lack the nervous system necessary for thought. They do not exhibit choice in how they act. At least some life forms fall outside of ethics then, and, in those cases, applying the NAP would be pointless even if you wanted to. At least this helps to narrow things down.

So the NAP does not apply to all animals, but even limiting the question to all animals with brains would not work, as some animals have evolved to eat only other animals with brains. Enforcing the NAP would mean death for them. It would only make sense to apply the NAP to creatures that could choose to follow it.

Originally, you thought that the NAP would apply to all humans, but it is not even true that humans always engage in purposeful behavior. Sometimes, people do things reflexively, like fainting. Sometimes, people do things unconsciously, like walking in their sleep. Sometimes, people do nothing at all, like those in comas. A person who suffers enough brain damage might have no thoughts whatsoever. They are no longer there, and their body is just an abandoned piece of property. This vegetative state happens when people die, but it can happen while the body is still alive if disease or an accident destroys their minds. That's why people designate agents to make medical decisions for them in case of emergencies. The mind cannot currently survive without the body, but the body can go on without the mind.

Someday, human minds might be transferable to machines, and the importance of the mind for ethics will be easier to understand. Being in a human body is not what matters. A human mind in a robot body would have the same ethical implications as an organic human. Similarly, artificial intelligence at least as sophisticated as a human mind would also fall under the NAP. Once AI reaches some threshold of complexity, it will step into ethical territory. Until then, it is fine that people create, change, and destroy computer programs. Eventually, though, libertarians may not be able to switch them off once they begin running. Some time after that, AI or other intelligent beings will likely far surpass biological human intelligence. No matter how intelligent, they will still engage in purposeful behavior. Hopefully, they will decide to abide by the non-aggression principle.

So being human is not important, per se. An extraordinarily intelligent animal that could do everything a human can do would be an ethical actor as well. Whatever form a mind takes, if it engages in behavior at least at the level of a human, then it makes sense to apply the non-aggression principle to it.

The NAP does not make any special distinction for humans or any group for that matter. It is the characteristics of the individual that determine whether they are ethical agents. The NAP does not include humans unless they meet the same criteria that a computer program or alien would need to meet. Very young, very old, very sick, or very injured humans might fall outside of ethical considerations depending on the condition of their mind. There would still be a host of moral concerns for how to deal with these people, but ethics would not be the right tool for the job and it is essential not to conflate the two.

You can only apply the NAP to beings that are engaging in purposeful behavior. If you apply the NAP to things that are not actors in the praxeological sense, then you will inevitably cause conflict with the real actors of the world. For example, if Annie wanted to protect a beautiful, old tree, she might say that the tree is an actor and chopping it down would be aggression. But the tree does not engage in purposeful behavior, so conflict cannot arise between it and someone. If she physically prevents you from felling the tree, she would not prevent a conflict but actually cause one. There are good ways of protecting such a tree, but misapplying the NAP is not one of them. Such misuse can promote conflict as much as failing to applying the NAP during real interactions between actors.

To make matters more complicated, merely characterizing an individual as ethically relevant can be misleading. Even normal adult humans engage in reflexive, instinctual behavior to some extent. So the question then becomes not who the NAP applies to but, for any individual, when does the NAP apply? Stated differently, the problem of classification is not whether an individual is ethically relevant, but whether any specific behavior is ethically relevant. It is a question of fact and something that you must evaluate on a case-by-case basis. Falling asleep might be intentional or unintentional, depending on the circumstances. You can make generalizations and find patterns, but there will always be exceptions. The NAP is a purely praxeological concept and makes no distinction based on who an actor is or to what group they belong.

Another way to think about this is whether praxeology is the best model to apply when trying to understand a particular behavior. For planets orbiting the sun, gravitational models work better. For insects responding to pheromones and babies crying when hungry, biological behavioral models work better. For adult humans plotting a course on a map, praxeology works best.

It may be that certain animals reach ethical relevance at some point in their lives. All animals bootstrap from ethically irrelevant cells into complex organisms and then eventually wither into ethical irrelevance. During this time, humans usually transition from engaging in no human action to doing it sometimes and then to doing it often. Tragically, some humans never develop minds that engage in human action during their lifetime, due to accidents or neurological disease. Similar tragedies might take a healthy adult human and remove their ability to engage in purposeful behavior. Like these marginal cases, many animals do not engage in purposeful behavior, and so never come under ethical consideration. Again, moral considerations may come into play but, from an ethical perspective, there is no possibility of conflict. You wonder where the great apes, dolphins, and other intelligent animals typically end up.

You ask your temporary neighbor if she thinks of her dog as a person.

"He thinks he is, that's for sure." When she sees you are serious, she thinks for a moment. "He's like a person in many ways. Definitely has personality. He's very clever at times. Then again, he sometimes gets these uncontrollable urges to destroy things. Not to mention he would probably eat himself to death if he ever got into the pantry. Such a fatty. I swear he can't be taught."

After so long on the brink of starvation, you can't blame the dog for seizing any opportunity to eat. You've been eating a lot lately as well, ever since you got to Freeport. You imagine you could train a dog not to overeat, but could you teach it to follow the NAP? It seems unlikely. The NAP requires concepts and understanding with which even humans struggle. But if a dog cannot understand the NAP, it can't be held liable for violating it. You cannot hold a creature to standards it cannot understand. If you do not hold it to ethical standards, it is also not afforded ethical protections.

Even if all animals were actors, the NAP would not make sense to some of them. For some animals, it seems quite right to eat each other. They cannot choose to follow the NAP and, without choice, there is no ethical agency. A world where you apply libertarianism to humans might be quite nice. Applied to animals, it would lead to death and chaos. You could kill an obligate carnivore by enforcing the NAP so they cannot eat, but you could not hunt them for food.

A similar problem arises for human societies that exist in extreme conditions like the arctic. They survive primarily on animal fat and protein and would die without hunting animals. Would it be ethical to stop them from doing so, even though they would all die? If killing animals violated the NAP, then Inuits are evil, and stopping them would not be. But if it is okay to kill certain animals for food in any scenario, then, in general, they have a different ethical status from humans.

You walk away from the pool and consider the ethical differences between various lifeforms and even artifical intelligence. Whenever anything engages in purposeful behavior it falls under the NAP. Any particular entity may sometimes do things purposefully and at other times reflexively. It is important to know when something is acting in the praxeological sense in order to avoid conflict, but the NAP does not give any clues as to how to identify purposeful behavior. An actor needs to do that itself, using its knowledge and understanding of the world.

You chance upon Big Billy, who is sitting in the street. He looks like he is talking to himself, but stops when you get closer. He is now wearing some shorts and a pair of sneakers.

"This place sucks," he says as you walk up. Nice to see you, too, you think to yourself.

"What's wrong?" you ask.

"I've been sitting here forever, and nobody will give me any money. I just need a little for food, can't they see I'm starving?"

"What about the money you got from selling your cargo?"

"I used it to buy these shoes." He looks down at his left sneaker and carefully brushes some dust off.

You look at the shoes. They seem fairly ordinary. You take a deep breath, open your mouth to say something, but then think better of it. Instead, you just say, "Maybe they noticed how nice your shoes are and figured that you can buy your own food."

"If I could, I would."

"You could get a job. Annie found some part-time work at one of the theaters."

"I don't want a job. I just want something to eat. It's not that complicated!"

"You could sell your shoes."

"Not going to happen."

"Well whatever you do, don't sell your ticket home."

Big Billy gives you a pathetic look.

You groan and say to him, "You have got to be kidding me."

"Look, I'm just down on my luck. Can I borrow some money? We've been through a lot together and I could really use the help. Please."

You think about it for what seems like only a few moments before Big Billy interrupts your thoughts.

"If you're not going to help me, just leave me alone." Big Billy licks his teeth. "I'll get out of here, one way or another."

You sigh and continue on your way.

David D. Friedman

"Producing laws is not an easier job than producing cars and food, so if the government is incompetent to produce cars or food, why do you expect it to do a good job producing the legal system within which you are then going to produce the cars and the food?"

SECURITY

Most people seem to stay inside during the afternoon, or at least stay in the shade. There is still some activity by one of the docks, so you head over to watch. A large ship is unloading containers. You cannot see what is inside them, but you occasionally hear people shouting about rice, so perhaps this is a food delivery. It must be hard to find fresh food, and you wonder if anyone here has ever gotten scurvy. Probably not, given the number of citrus trees growing in front of almost every other building.

You see some smaller ships unloading cargo as well. Many goods are coming in, but nothing is going out. You make a mental note to ask someone if Freeport exports anything. Then you head back into the center of town. You've become familiar with some of the main paths through the city and can identify a few landmarks here and there, though you still need to ask for directions occasionally.

Eventually, you find Annie chatting with Chelsea. You wander over to listen to their conversation.

"So I tell them, 'Be excellent to each other!'" you hear Chelsea say as you walk up. Annie laughs.

"So how does your company deal with people dumping trash into the ocean? Everyone here is producing garbage every day. Do they just toss it overboard? Doesn't the wind blow a lot of trash into the water?" Annie asks.

"That kind of pollution is illegal here."

"I don't remember that being on the list."

"Yeah, the list is just something I made up. In an anarcho-capitalist society like this one, the real rule is the non-aggression principle. If you follow the NAP, then you are just fine. But for most people, it is easier to think about in terms of more specific crimes. I would guess that some of the people don't even know what the non-aggression principle is. But everyone knows what stealing is."

"So what about pollution?" Annie asks.

"Yeah, we don't like pollution here, but it's a little tricky. Pollution isn't necessarily a crime, just like killing isn't necessarily a crime. A month or so ago a woman was attacked by someone who was visiting. We found out later that he tried to drug her at a restaurant. When that didn't work, he waited for her near her home with a rag soaked in general anesthetic. She was able to push him away, but then he tried to strangle her. She ended up pulling a concealed handgun and shooting him three times. He died twenty minutes later. She suffered a broken collar bone and some bruising but was otherwise unharmed. At least physically. The psychological damage is another story."

"That's awful."

"I know, but it gets worse. It turned out that the man had made travel plans for both him and his "wife". We'll never know what he was planning, but I'm sure it gives the lady nightmares. Anyway, that is my roundabout way of explaining that killing isn't always a crime. Same thing for pollution. Now, if people go dumping chemicals into the ocean, and those chemicals get in the fish, and then someone eats the fish and gets sick, you better believe that's a crime. That's like sneaking into a restaurant and poisoning the food. It's the same thing with smoke or trash. If it ends up on someone else's property, that's a problem. On the other hand, if they gently reincorporate it into the natural environment, nobody here is going to bat an eye. Especially if they don't see it."

"If no one sees it, it didn't happen?" Annie asks.

"More like, if it doesn't hurt anyone or cause any problems down the line, then it probably isn't aggression. But even if something isn't poison, if it ruins the aesthetic of the community, that is still a problem. There was a kid who would dump his dinner into the water because he didn't like the food. If it had sunk and been eaten by fish, that would have been fine. But the stuff floated and stuck to the sides of people's boats and sections. It didn't cause any damage, but you can't deface property like that. Not the most glamorous case, but I solved it." Chelsea pats herself on the back.

"But what about things that might cause damage 'down the line' like building up toxins in the food chain or pollutants that build up in the atmosphere? It might take a long time to feel the effects of those things."

"It doesn't matter when the harm happens. It is still aggression if you are causing the problem. And you don't have to wait for things to get really bad. If you can see that someone is doing something wrong that will lead to big problems down the line, you can stop them, just like you can stop someone who hasn't hurt you yet, but is drunk and walking toward you swinging a knife.

"It doesn't matter if the culprit is one man or a big corporation. Libertarianism doesn't make exceptions, so it's the best system for protecting the environment. Another reason is that the wealthier people are the more time they have to worry about the environment. If you really care about the environment, then you should promote libertarianism.

"Also, the point of avoiding pollution isn't just to keep everyone here happy. We have to worry about our reputation with outsiders. That's one of the reasons why section owners and businesses are contractually obligated to be extra careful with waste and pollution. Many people would like to send us to the bottom of the ocean, and many so-called environmentalists are more than happy to raze our city if they think it will stop humans from eating fish or peeing in the water. Well, do you know who else eats fish and pees in the water? Pretty much every animal in the ocean."

Chelsea shakes her head. "Anyway, from one perspective, you can say that any living being is constantly polluting the environment just by breathing. But breathing doesn't usually interfere with anyone else's business, so don't worry about it. While you are here, at least."

"So where do you draw the line? I saw a lady sweeping dust and dirt into the ocean. I'm guessing she doesn't get prosecuted for that."

"Of course not. The security companies have come up with shared guidelines for common questions based on cases they have already had to resolve. Those documents are all public, so you could read about it if you like. I follow their guidelines unless somebody points out unusual circumstances, or I notice something that seems like a crime. But yeah, sweeping dust or dried salt into the ocean isn't usually considered a crime. Even for situations that are likely crimes, I don't just act on my own unless it is an emergency. Normally, I first make a report to my company, and if they think it is worth pursuing, then I have to ask a judge and get their opinion. Based on what they think, then I'll start trying to set things right."

"What if someone does something wrong? How do you deal with criminals after you catch them?"

"Oh, I don't do much. I just put a stop to any conflicts and write a report. My company then submits a report to the relevant insurance companies, who work out appropriate restitution with a judge. Usually, the criminal has to pay the victim some money. If things go badly, I might get involved in ejecting someone from the city or delinking their section, but that is rare. Usually, people pay up."

"How do they determine how much?"

"I'm not sure, but I've heard that they try to use market mechanisms. I know that some of the info comes from insurance companies when they price out policies against accidental aggression. Some comes from police companies like the one I work for when we submit invoices for different jobs. There's also a secondary market for judgments. All of it helps us find good amounts for restitution.

"I hear about huge awards given in other places around the world for the stupidest stuff. All I can think is that it can't be justice. One of the principles my company lives by is proportionality. Do enough to make things right but don't go too far. I know everyone has different opinions and you can't put a one-size-fits-all monetary value on stepping on someone's foot. Some people might brush it off, or at most want an apology. Other people might hate getting stepped on and would require some additional compensation. But, in general, the company has figured out rough guidelines for what people in our society expect, and a judge usually adjusts from there based on the circumstances."

Annie breaks in, "But why do the expectations in a society matter? Shouldn't it just be based on something objective?"

"I'm not sure that is possible. You never really have the same situation twice. Even if you did, the people involved might have radically different subjective experiences. What they go through emotionally is part of why they should get compensation. A robbery might be emotionally difficult for some people. Others might just want their property back."

"Okay, but if everything is different, then how do you figure it out at all?" Annie asks.

"I think there was some back and forth about this a few years ago. You know, if you are a victim, you want the restitution to be as high as possible. If you are a criminal, you want it to be as low as possible. But throughout life, everyone is capable of being a victim or a criminal under certain circumstances. Nobody is perfect. So what people really want are reasonable, proportional judgments.

"Nobody is going to sign up for our protection if we don't guarantee a decent level of restitution. The same thing goes for insurance. On the other hand, nobody is going to sign up to have unrealistic liabilities. So it is a balancing act that requires market forces to figure out. To some extent, we can rely on historical decisions. That's a start, and then the pressure from the market drives judgments toward generally reasonable and socially acceptable levels. Those levels won't match what everyone wants or expects, but arbiters can make adjustments, depending on who is involved."

"So the various companies involved set their own guidelines based on consumer demand? What if the market decides that assault doesn't warrant restitution? Then nobody would prosecute assailants? Assault is always a violation of the NAP."

"Well, the point of restitution is to try to restore things to how they would have been if the conflict had never occurred. That's not completely possible, but sometimes you can tie some physical metrics to it. Like if someone steals your bike, then returning the bike is part of restitution. Fungible goods like gold coins are even easier. However, if you kill someone, we can't bring them back, so we have to estimate how much money that person's life is worth. It's a tricky thing to do. Same thing with emotional damage, pain, suffering, and other subjective things that result from crime.

"I think they try to be as quantitative as possible, and then use judgment for the rest. Ultimately, I think arbiters start with their company's restitution guidelines and then adjust based on the details of the situation."

"Don't courts everywhere work that way?" Annie asks.

"Many courts work that way but, in other places, justice is one of many goals, and not always the top one."

Annie gives you a look that says she is skeptical about Chelsea's exposition of legal theory. Then you see her expression become quizzical again.

"What about accidents?" Annie asks.

"What about them?"

"If someone accidentally breaks something, is that a crime?"

"Usually, but less of a crime than if they do it on purpose."

"Why does intention matter?"

"Oh, it matters a lot. If a kid breaks something on purpose, I know that they are probably going to do it again, or get into other sorts of trouble. Maybe that's why people are usually more forgiving if it is an accident. They don't feel violated as with intentional crimes. Also, I don't have to worry about locking them up to keep people safe."

"You put people in prison?"

"We don't have an actual prison here, at least not what most people think of as one. We have a few holding cells, but it is only for temporarily restraining people. If we need to separate someone from society for a long time, we exile them."

"Exile?"

"Yes, they have to leave. Depending on the crime, they can leave on a boat if they can afford passage, or we can drop them off the next time we pass land."

"Is imprisonment against libertarianism?"

"I don't think so, but it's too expensive for a small city like ours. Who wants to pay to feed, house, and clothe a criminal for 60 years? I imagine a larger libertarian society would have prisons. Maybe some wealthy philanthropist would decide to fund it as a charitable endeavor. Someone could probably build a business model around it if there were enough criminals. We're lucky not to have that problem, so neither has happened here yet."

"What if someone is too dangerous to let go?"

"Well, there is always capital punishment. It's something that has only ever been used by individuals trying to protect themselves, never by companies after the fact. I don't know if others would agree with me when I use the term capital punishment for situations where someone defends themselves from would-be rapists and murderers. Anyway, I could imagine an extreme situation where a judge would consider it justified to put someone to death. There is nothing un-libertarian about killing per se, but it is such a risky course of action. If you make a mistake, you can't fix it. So, you can't use it for every little crime, and it's hard to use it for big ones as well. And then there is the fact that even if you could justify it, the victims might not agree with it. So yeah, it's complicated."

Chelsea checks the time and says she has to get going. After she heads off, you and Annie decide to start walking toward a park. You chat a bit about her part-time job and some of the local people whom she has met. She has been making friends easily, and you feel a pang of jealousy. When the two of you arrive at the park later, you see Dirk sitting alone. Annie gets a mischievous look on her face and heads over to him.

"Hey Dirk, long time no see."

"Hello, Annie. If you do not mind, I am a bit busy at the moment."

"I don't mind at all," Annie says, sitting down next to him.

Dirk looks like he is about to protest, but he straightens his bow tie and asks, "What can I help you with?"

"Oh, my friend here wanted to ask you a few questions."

You shoot a look at Annie, but she asks her own question without waiting.

"Why do you think a government hasn't tried to attack you? They have big militaries that could easily take over this place."

"Easily?" Dirk looks a bit prickly.

"Unless you have some invisible army hidden somewhere."

"No, you are right that we are no match in a fight. There are many military ships that could by themselves kill everyone here and sink every last section to the bottom of the ocean. But we know that, so why would we fight?"

"You would just let anyone take over?"

"Why would they want to take us over? Most navy ships have no interest in Freeport. We are not a threat to anyone. Nor are we a hazard. We stay out of territorial waters and shipping lanes. When Freeport was new, an occasional military ship would ask us what we were doing and if we needed help. Now, they do not even bother radioing to talk to us. We have noticed the occasional UAV flying over for a look but, in general, they do not care.

"Even if someone wanted to attack, there would not be much to gain from it. Say they sail in with a bunch of ships and force Freeport into submission. Then what? Set up taxes and regulations? If they do that, people will not want to live here. The city would vanish. The sections are all independent craft, and if they did not scatter to the wind within a month, then I am sure the people would."

"What if they just wanted to kill you?" Annie persists.

"There certainly are politicians who like to kill people for glory or just do it to get their cronies military contracts. But, in our case, it seems like the incentives are not there. We do not have a military or natural resources. So, unless they made up some horrible story about us, it would be difficult for them to get political support, let alone convince a military commander to murder a few thousand civilians in cold blood. I have met many good soldiers who would disobey that order without hesitation."

Dirk continues, "That said, even if nobody is shooting at us, we are still under attack. Not just in the media, where our reputation is constantly under fire, but even here."

Annie looks around.

"Not directly, that is, but cyberattacks hit our networks frequently. Our internet connectivity is less than ideal to begin with, especially when we are far from land, but more often than not, someone is trying to break into local networks here or run denial-of-service attacks against us. Our internet service providers try their best, but there is only so much they can do. So even if a state is not sending its navy after us, they might still mean us harm. It may not seem important whether we can get online, but staying connected to the rest of the world is part of how we stay safe."

"So how do you handle dealing with other governments?" Annie asks.

"Other?" Dirk asks curtly. He looks offended this time.

"Sorry, I didn't mean it like that."

"We are just a company that owns an oversized tugboat. Our goal is to make a profit by serving our customers. Our best strategy is to stay in international waters and avoid governments like the plague."

"What about trading?" Annie asks.

"That is all handled by the individual companies who are engaged in trade. We do not get involved."

"How does that work? Other countries just let companies based in Freeport bring in goods?" she asks.

"Other?" Dirk asks with a smirk. This time he is merely amused.

"Sorry," Annie says with a grin.

"Each country has its own rules about trade and what kind of inspections and certifications they need for imports and exports. Most countries are happy to let the companies in their territory sell us whatever they want, excepting goods and services with military value. We would be hard-pressed to import military aircraft, but I am not sure what we would do with something like that. Nobody has attached a landing strip section yet. Even if we had a military aircraft, nobody would want it on their section. It would just be an expensive bullseye.

"Many countries are more restrictive when it comes to imports. Some of them ban people from trading with us at all. It is sad when that happens. They have an opportunity to work together with us and become wealthier, but they completely waste it."

"So Freeport does not restrict what people can bring here?" Annie asks.

"Not specific items, but the contracts with our customers require them to keep certain levels of insurance. Most of the local insurance companies will not insure you if you are transporting dangerous things, at least not at affordable prices, so people tend not to bring things that will cause problems."

"What about things that are illegal?"

"Illegal where? We do not care too much about what is illegal in other places. When other cities ban peaceful products like recreational drugs, they create a black market for smugglers. Do not misunderstand me. Those smugglers are doing good work by providing goods that people otherwise would not have been able to enjoy. The downside is that these hidden channels also create avenues for unethical activities like theft and trading in stolen goods. So as much as I support the efforts of smugglers, Freeport does not arbitrarily restrict what someone imports or exports. Not only is it cost-effective, but it also allows us to focus on more important things."

"Like what?"

"Since the only things that are illegal here are violations of the non-aggression principle, we do not have to worry about peaceful people trying to sneak in peaceful products. We only worry about stopping aggression. So people cannot bring stolen goods here and try to fence them. And we put a stop to any human trafficking, child abuse media, and other crime-related material. It is sickening that those trades exist at all, but we have taught people the hard way not to try that here at least."

"What about goods that are produced with or subsidized by taxes? You don't allow taxation here, but would you allow the import of goods produced by governments?" Annie asks. "If part of the input is tainted, then the output is tainted as well, right?"

"That is insightful. Unfortunately, governments have subsidized virtually all of the goods traded in the world in some fashion. Governments have also beleaguered them with regulations and taxes. So now, we face a continuum problem. On one end, we have a carpenter who was taxed, and then some of that tax money was used to subsidize his hammer. I do not see any problem with buying his goods. On the other end, you have someone with a government-granted monopoly selling furniture that was made by slaves using tools that were entirely paid for by taxes. In that case, I would say, and local arbiters agree with me, that their goods are as bad as stolen. The police do not let people sell things they steal in Freeport, and they do not let them sell things they steal from other places around the world either. Unfortunately, most trade goods are somewhere in between, and we do not have a good way of determining exactly where they lie. That is the nature of continuum problems, though. People ask you where the threshold is when no threshold exists at all. We merely try to use good judgment.

"It is as if I were to say that lightly tapping someone is okay, but punching them hard is not, so where do you draw the line? The truth is you cannot even say that a light tap is never aggression and a heavy punch is always aggression. Statistically, they may be more or less likely, but you cannot create a rule based on how hard someone is hitting someone else. Have you met the woman who runs the Freeport newsletter?"

Annie shakes her head.

"Right. I am used to the bad old days when we were small, and everyone knew everyone. Well, she told me she was thinking of starting a rating service for just this kind of question. Business owners could pay to have their products certified as being produced ethically. There is definitely a market for it here, but I wonder if it would catch on in other places around the world. I hope she gets it off the ground."

Annie moves on to the next thing on her mind. "I have heard that people come here for a better economic life. Are there many political refugees as well?"

Dirk gives her a weary look. "Most people come here for work, though many have also come to escape some oppressive society or regime. Occasionally, criminals from other parts of the world think they can hide out here. We have zero tolerance for crime in general, so you can imagine our typical reaction to being put at risk by criminals who think they can use us as a shield against governments."

"You turn them over to the government?"

"No. We prosecute them for endangering the people of Freeport by making this city a target. If you pull a lion's tail and then hide behind someone, you are liable if the lion eats them. Well, we do not let things get that far. The same thing applies to individuals who want to use Freeport as a secret hideout for committing crimes online. To be here, you need to follow the rule. Otherwise, we have to go our separate ways."

"That said," he continues, "we have had real criminals show up before, looking for a place to hide. We sent them back to face justice, or at least whatever passes for justice in their homeland. It is not a perfect solution, but it is the best we can do at this point.

"Then, there are the unfortunate who have not done anything wrong from our perspective but are being pursued by some government. They come here because they think we can protect them from this or that government, but there is nothing we can do for them. Instead, they only endanger the rest of us. We kick them out of the city and wish them good luck.

"Of course, that is only how things are now. One day, I hope that—I know that—we will get to a point where there are large libertarian societies that can stand up to governments. They will be able to grant asylum to people targeted by states. At that point, everyone will have a real choice about how they want to live, and not have to make trade-offs between liberty and capital. I think the incentives will be very compelling, and people will stampede away from their tax farms to the wild, green pastures of libertarian anarchy."

Dirk looks wistful for a moment.

"Until then, people with the means to emigrate still have the choice about what kind of aggression they would like to suffer. Would you prefer to live under a government that steals more of your money or one that punishes you for your personal life choices? If you can move, you can at least make things a little more to your liking. We are lucky that there is not a single world government, because people would not even have that choice.

"That is another reason I am hesitant to get involved around the world. If you get involved in a conflict between two people, you might be able to help. But millions? You end up in the same position as government bureaucrats who try to come up with one-size-fits-all solutions to everything."

Dirk turns to you.

"Well, if Annie has finished with her questions, perhaps we can get to yours," he says.

You didn't have a question, but after thinking for a moment you ask, "So what can we do?"

"Governments are not independently powerful. They cannot exist without the support of people. They give people an incentive to support them, either financially, emotionally, or with thinly veiled threats. However, I think the best way to get rid of government is to give people better options. Ideally, that would be liberty right where they currently live. That is hard, though. Another avenue would be a wealthy, libertarian society for like-minded people to move to, but that is far off and still difficult for people who do not want to give up their family and friends. So in the short run, I am bullish on agorism, which means people finding free-market options for areas in which the government is meddling. When governments ban alcohol, people create speakeasies. When governments spy on communications, people create better and better encryption.

"If you give people superior alternatives to the state, they will choose to use them. When a large number of people look around and realize that the state is irrelevant, it will die. Not with a bloody revolution but with a yawn.

"We do not even need to convince everyone. Most people go along with whatever everyone else is doing. A few million libertarians could lead a peaceful revolution and change the world. And once a former country or two are free..."

Dirk trails off, shakes his head, and rubs his eyes. "I enjoy thinking about it, but we still have much work to do. Excuse me, but I need to get some rest. Have a good evening."

He walks off and leaves, you and Annie alone in the park. You sit together and chat until Annie says that she has a meeting she needs to attend. After she leaves you head back to your hotel to get some sleep.

Walking back, you realize that your feelings are in a strange juxtaposition. On the one hand, you are in a place that is surrounded by potential enemies. An entire world of governments, most having both the means and disposition to crush a budding anarchy. From that perspective, it does not seem safe to be here. On the other hand, the city itself has a peaceful order to it. They take great care to protect liberty, and they serve justice when things go wrong. Crime rates are lower here than most places with governments. From that perspective, this is one of the safest places you could be.

With an ocean between you and the nearest government, you decide that you are probably safe and secure. You head back to your room, indulge in a long shower, and fall asleep with ease.

Ludwig von Mises

"Government means always coercion and compulsion and is by necessity the opposite of liberty."

AGGRESSION

Your bed rips out from under you, and you land on the floor. There is a ringing in your ears, and it takes you a minute of groping before you can get up and look around your tiny hotel room. You wonder if Freeport crashed into land. The view from your small window is dark, so you get dressed and go outside to look around.

It is late at night, but the moon is full, so it is easy enough to walk around. A siren goes off. A few people are running about, but most people seem to be staying inside. Something in the back of your mind tells you to go back to your hotel room and wait but, after a moment of hesitation, you decide to continue looking around. Maybe there is someone who needs help.

You head toward the center of the city. After some time, you recognize Dirk in a hurry to get somewhere. You run over to him and match his pace.

"What is going on?" you ask him.

"Why are you out here? Go back to your room and stay inside."

You hear a bang in the direction of your hotel. You start to wonder if Freeport is the real Danger Island. Dirk stops for a moment to listen and then looks at you.

"Shit, never mind, come with me." He takes you into a nearby building and slams the door shut. "Stay away from the windows," he says.

Inside is some sort of office full of screens and electronic equipment. There are live camera feeds from all around Freeport. Some of them seem to be aerial views from high above the city.

A young man turns to Dirk and says, "Someone cut the power to two of our X-bands, so we didn't see them until they were right up on us."

"Just one ship?" Dirk asks.

The young man nods.

"No AIS transponder?"

"No."

"Pirates. Any trespassers?"

"None reported. We've heard explosions, but haven't had any reports of injuries or damage, aside from the sabotage."

"Good. Deploy the beholders." Dirk relaxes visibly and sits down. Someone hands him a cup of tea.

"Are those a type of weapon?"

Dirk laughs and shakes his head. "No, they are just mobile buoys with video cameras on top. They do not have any weapons on them."

"How does that help with pirates?"

"Pirates are generally looking for easy prey. They do not want a fight any more than we do. They think if they can scare us they can get some tribute. We have worked hard to disabuse the pirates of the world of that notion, but someone keeps spreading rumors that the reason pirates leave us alone is that we always secretly pay them off. If I ever find out who is broadcasting those lies, I am going to return the favor twice over."

Dirk looks stern for a moment, then softens.

"Anyway, you came at a bad time. Did you know that this part of the world has one of the highest concentrations of piracy?"

You shake your head.

"Well, do not worry too much. Our law enforcement companies would not have much trouble defending us from a medium-sized pirate ship like this one. I am surprised that they are threatening us at all. When Freeport was much smaller, it would happen occasionally. But as we got larger, and the numbers of ships in tow grew, pirates became scarce. We have some residents who are not officially part of any security organization but would jump at the chance to defend the city. There are one or two who are real weapon enthusiasts who could probably give a group like that a run for their money. We do not want any fighting to happen, so I sometimes worry more about them than the pirates. It has never come to that, thankfully. Social pressure is all you need. And as a matter of policy, we prefer to resolve conflicts like this without violence whenever possible. It is much better for business."

"If you're not going to fight, how will you win?"

"Well, if they set foot on Freeport, then there will be blood. But if we are lucky, then they will only be dumb enough to threaten us from afar, not so suicidally stupid that they might try to invade. I expect we will only need to use a simple strategy that has worked well in the past."

"What is that?"

"First, we broadcast live videos and commentary about what is going on, so the whole world knows who the bad guys are. Drones and cameras are cheap these days. We send pictures and videos of their ship, their faces, and any other information about who they are and from where they came. I have someone taking photographs as we speak. It is dark now, but as soon as the sun comes up, everyone will see them for who they are. Every time they aggress against us, we will document it and share it with the world."

"Then what?"

"In the past, if state authorities were already seeking them, then someone would often come and collect them."

"And if that doesn't work?"

"Then we use the greatest weapon of all." He smiles and pauses for effect. "Money."

"I thought you have a no-pay policy for pirates."

"The money is not for them. We offer a bounty on their ship and their crew. They do not always get caught, but they almost always get scared off."

"That works?"

"Usually. We even had a pirate pay his bounty once. That was fun!"

"If you have the firepower to take out an enemy ship, why bother with cameras and bounties? Wouldn't it be cheaper to sink it and move on with your lives?"

"Perhaps in the short run, but we have a reputation to protect. If pirates start to think we are combative, I worry that instead of using scare tactics like they are now, they will be much more aggressive and start hurting people. More importantly, you would be surprised how much it matters what people think of us. We do not have any support out here in international waters. There is no one we can appeal to for help during an attack or justice afterward. Since we do not fly the flag of any country, warships and other government ships from any state can board us without international consequences. We're not recognized as a separate entity by any country, so the best we can hope for is to be ignored. People from many different countries live here, so we are at risk of falling afoul of more laws than we could ever track. We have to keep a low profile. Furthermore, trade is our lifeblood, and if we become known for resorting to violence, even if we can justify it as self-defense, our merchants will have a hard time buying and selling around the world. What is worse is that certain people and organizations will take any excuse to cast us in a bad light. We have to be hyper-vigilant not to give them any ammunition.

"Not to mention that the danger and risk of serious injury will make people reluctant to live here. It is hard enough to get people to give up their lives and move to another city, let alone one that wanders around the oceans. We have made so much progress, and I worry that if our population drops, we will lose our momentum and it will be hard to recover."

The young man comes back and reports, "We tried to get some photos with a telescopic lens, but haven't gotten anything useful yet. It's still too dark, and their crew is being unusually disciplined about staying inside and out of sight."

When he steps away, you continue interrogating Dirk. "What do you do when the bounties don't work?"

"It has only happened once before. We were much smaller back then. The pirates, we later found out, were a group of young men from Indonesia. They were not especially brave. They just had not heard of us before and did not have the sense to use any of the communication equipment on their ship. We sent a speed boat to try to explain the situation, but they ended up shooting at it. Nobody got hurt, thankfully."

"So what did you do?"

"Well, Freeport had quite a few people who wanted to sink the pirate ship. Their vessel was a stolen fishing boat, so it seemed easy enough. But then another group came forward with a solution that would solve the problem and at the same time protect our reputation. As you can imagine, we have a large number of people here who enjoy scuba diving. I am a certified rescue diver myself. Anyway, a few of them volunteered to gear up and sabotage the pirate ship.

"We thought it would be easy. Though, like everything on a seastead, it was harder than we expected. We almost lost someone. But, thanks to some creative thinking and heroic effort, the team disabled the enemy propulsion system. After that, the pirates slowly drifted away. Of course, we never advertised our little operation so that we could keep it in the playbook, so to speak."

"A single pirate ship is one thing, but what would you do if a government came after you?"

"A government is just a larger, more powerful pirate armada. I am not looking forward to the day when we have to face one. We obviously would not resort to violence. That is government's forte, and we would not stand a chance. As you can imagine, bounties will not work either. So we would have to rely on PR plays, blackmail if we have any leverage, and to some extent business connections. Sometimes our investors can intervene on our behalf."

"Investors?"

"Yes. Freeport is a business. The company manages the cores to which everyone else is connected."

"So how does the business make money?"

"The cores are what we use to anchor Freeport or slowly move it around the globe. We charge a monthly fee for being connected, though people closer to a core typically have long-term contracts."

"How is that different from property taxes?"

"The difference is that you do not have to pay anything if you do not want to. And even if you do not pay anything, you do not have to leave. We have quite a few ships that stick with us but never attach directly to the city. I am not sure how much money they end up saving since they have to pay for their fuel, but that is up to them.

"Not to mention that many residents are also stockholders in the company. When we do well, they do well. Most section owners generate much more money with their businesses than they pay in connection fees. Some of them even make their money back just from what they charge our company. We are, in a sense, paying them to be connected."

"Like the police?"

"Right."

"How do you control the arrangement of different sections?"

"It is all based on individual contracts with our customers. It is considered valuable to be close to popular sections like parks, so people contract with us and with the sections that they want to be close to for guaranteed relative placement. Some sections value being on the border so they can maintain docks for tourism, fishing, import, and export business. It has been interesting to see the city evolve. When we anchor, there are often rearrangements, especially on the outskirts."

"Isn't it dangerous to move the city around? My old ship almost got torn apart by ocean waves, and the weather wasn't even that bad."

"It is risky to move, but it is not safe to stay in one place either. Bad weather is the most overt threat, but saltwater destroys our hulls. The bacteria in the ocean do as well. Wind, waves, and animals are all continually wearing down our boats and modules. Did you know that when two different metals are near each other in saltwater, it creates an electrical potential that corrodes one of them? I learned it in chemistry class, but it never occurred to me that it happens to ships until I started living here. We have learned the hard way to be careful with the ocean. We have good data about wind and weather patterns, as well as which areas of the ocean have rough water. We tend to stay near the equator and move from safe harbor to safe harbor. I think Freeport could handle a small hurricane or two, but I have no intention of testing that theory."

"So you control who can be here and how much to charge for membership. How is that different from a government?"

Dirk looks pained at the comparison but maintains a smile. "The primary difference is that government takes taxes by force and unilaterally decides what services to provide. People call it the social contract, but that is just a cover story. Another way of saying it is that government is a criminal organization, and there is no justification for the way it does things. Freeport, on the other hand, has explicit, written contracts for services, with explicit fees and conditions. Everyone who agrees to the contract can read it first, and there are mechanisms for exiting the contract if either party is no longer satisfied with the arrangement. Being a part of Freeport is voluntary. Being the subject of a government is not."

"What about kids that are born here? They don't have a choice."

"Children do not have any obligations. Even when they become adults, there is nothing that obligates them to contract with our company or any other company. Someone could live their whole life in Freeport without entering into any contracts. With taxes, the government takes them no matter what."

"Some people don't seem to mind paying taxes."

"Yes, but they are not given a choice. They are not deciding whether to pay taxes or not. They are deciding whether to pay taxes or go to jail. The fact that government has to threaten people to get them to comply is evidence that many people would not participate if they truly had the option. Good ideas do not require force."

"So people can just leave here whenever they want?"

"Yes, and they often do. Some sections can move around on their own. Even if they cannot, every time we get near a city, a few get towed away and one or two new ones join. There are advantages to being stationary, so we like to give our customers the option to disconnect when we can."

"Isn't that bad for business?"

"We do lose a little revenue when someone departs. But people are much more likely to join if they know it is easy to leave. We try to do anything that increases the value of our services, and an easy out is considered valuable.

"We may not like it when customers decide to leave, but increasing our population cannot come at any cost. Freedom of association works both ways, and the company reserves the right to eject people who cause trouble. They are still free to tag along if they like. You may have noticed some ships that sail along with us under their own power. But most people either choose to stay connected or sail off into the sunset."

"And if someone doesn't want to leave?"

"If they committed a crime, we hire one of the police companies to take care of them."

"Chelsea said that the police are private. Isn't that dangerous? The competing police companies might disagree on something and end up fighting."

"They could, but that would be very expensive. Any police company that would tend toward violence instead of competition would have higher costs and lower profits. That goes not just for violence against other companies, but against the people of Freeport as well. More peaceful companies would out-compete them. That is the theory, anyway. In practice, they never fight. Instead, they occasionally work together to some extent to save on costs.

"But we would not want them to be too friendly, either. Competition between the police agencies means they keep an eye on each other. It is easy to take market share if you expose a competing security company doing something unethical. On the other hand, if you have one monopoly police force, then the police can commit crimes without facing any consequences. It is a common problem all over the world. How many stories have you heard of police stealing, killing, or even framing people for crimes that they did not commit? Having multiple competing companies keeps the police honest. Just the fact that someone *could* create a competing company helps keep them in check."

"And the arbitration companies, what do they do if they disagree about something?"

"They hire an arbitration company."

"But..." you trail off and think about it for a bit. So instead of having a monopoly court that has the final say, they have to resolve their differences through arbitration. Hmm.

Dirk grins at your thoughtful expression.

"What if someone doesn't want to do what an arbitrator says?"

"If you take someone's computer, and the arbitrator decides that you stole it and that it should be returned, then not returning it can have bad consequences for you. First, the police would probably take it from you anyway, so it would get returned. Second, the compensation determined by an arbitrator generally assumes that the parties will be cooperative. If you are non-cooperative, you might incur additional damages, since resisting justice creates additional injustices. Finally, and perhaps most importantly, people will find out that you did not abide by the arbitrator's ruling. No security company will contract with you. Without either a good reputation or a security firm, most businesses will not hire you. Most residential companies will not rent or sell to you, either. The market begins to disassociate from you, and life quickly becomes more difficult and expensive."

"That's fine for actual criminals, but what if an arbitrator makes a mistake? Or someone is best friends with an arbitrator and gets them to always rule in their favor? An innocent person might lose everything."

"Abusing your position as an arbitrator is a crime, so the victim could take the arbitrator to arbitration."

"It seems like this chain of arbitrations might never end."

"And that is okay. The only correct place to end is with justice, or as close as we can get. If you have a monopoly court system with one ultimate decision maker, then you have no recourse when that ultimate decision maker makes a mistake. Justice can never get served. It is easy for an anarchist to generalize and say the government is bad and we should get rid of it, but the truth is that many of the things government does are good. It just does them poorly, and there is no way for a government system to do them well. This would be tolerable if government were monopolizing and ruining something superfluous like wrapping paper, but police and courts are an essential part of society. It is so important to do them well, and yet they are the last things people think to privatize."

"But if private companies are in charge of everything, won't they exploit people?"

"You must see by now, it is the government that exploits people. It uses aggression to take what it wants, forces people to do what it wants, and tries to destroy anyone who resists. In contrast, companies do not have arbitrary power. It is only with government that you are guaranteed continual and pervasive aggression. So the question is not whether companies will use aggression, but in which system people will enjoy more liberty."

Then, Dirk turns and looks at some of the new video feeds coming back over the displays. He squints and mutters something to himself.

"Hey," he calls to his assistant, "come look at this."

The younger man walks over.

"These are not pirates. That is a French military ship. P400, right?"

The ship is hard to see in the dark, but the young man agrees. He spends some time at a computer and then announces, "it is most likely a ship owned by the Kenya Navy."

"Has something like this ever happened before?" you ask.

"It is not the first time we have had to deal with a government ship, though it is the first time that a government ship has been confrontational. I am not sure what to make of that. Do we have something they want?" Dirk trails off.

"Why did they attack us?" you ask.

"I do not know. It does not make sense. Perhaps they want us to shoot back so they can claim we fired first. Hopefully, that means they have not officially reported anything, and we still might be able to resolve this peacefully. Depending on who put them up to it." Dirk says to the young man, "Try again to get them on the radio. If they do not respond, we will wait and see what they do next. And make sure there is not anyone else out there who might be pulling a fast one on us."

Half an hour goes by without any news or noise outside. You break the silence with a question.

"If there were a place like Freeport on land, would you move there?"

Dirk does not hesitate. "Of course. It would be much easier. Certainly safer." Dirk tilts his head at the image of the Kenya Navy ship. "And, of course, much cheaper. Most people do not think about our finances, but Freeport is incredibly expensive to operate. Having no government saves us money by allowing the proper allocation of societal resources, but having no government on land would be even more cost-effective. So, yes, I suspect if we achieved anarchy on solid ground, that would likely be the siren song for my final voyage. Not everyone, though. Many of our customers love the sea. I imagine they would purchase the company and its assets. Freeport would live on, but likely with a much smaller population. I would still come and visit, though."

"But even if it meant that Freeport would die, you would leave?"

"A city is not what we are trying to build. We are trying to engender a state of mind—a world where people value freedom and choose to respect liberty. People look at the material things we have built and think that is our achievement. It is nothing. The future we are all looking forward to has nothing to do with specific places or technologies. What we want to create is much greater than that. A world where people are as free as they can be."

"A world where liberty is the norm?"

"Yes, but liberty is not enough. I want liberty and capital. Our customers do, too. When Freeport was just getting started, we could not convince anyone to come. Total liberty, but no supermarkets. No taxes, but no jobs either. Low crime rates, but low dating prospects. It took a long time before we had the things people wanted. Even today, we do not have everything."

Dirk gets a wry look on his face, but it fades as the young man returns with a worried look. This time he whispers to Dirk. Both of them look at a screen and then look at you.

"Care to explain this?" Dirk asks.

He turns the screen toward you, and you see a video of a man pulling the wires out of some electronic equipment. You cannot see his face, but the sneakers and bandanna are an unmistakable fashion statement. You curse under your breath.

"He tried to break into one of the cores, but could not get in. The last footage we have of him shows him stealing a small but expensive boat. That was about four hours ago."

Dirk tightens his jaw and looks at you.

"I have no idea what is going on," you tell him.

He says nothing for a moment, and then, "We do not have time for this. Keep our guest comfortable but under guard in another room until..."

The young man interrupts, "Sorry, sir, the ship finally responded to us." He puts a hand on his earpiece and pauses for a moment. "Here is what they said." He plays a recording, and you hear a radio transmission in vaguely British English: "You are hereby ordered to change course. You will anchor this vessel at Mombasa. You have one hour to comply." The message repeats several times.

"We asked them what this was about, and they sent over this audio recording."

Next, you hear Big Billy's voice. "They captured me and my ship. They wouldn't give me any food. I was starving. I think they were going to sell me into slavery. It's a slave trade."

A low growl starts to boil in the back of Dirk's throat.

"Has it been posted to the internet?" Dirk asks quickly.

"Not as far as we can tell."

Dirk speaks rapidly to the young man, "Ask to parley. If they agree, I will meet them at the halfway point on a speedboat and try to work something out. Get me a tablet with footage of our former guest, any information you can find on the Kenyan crew, and a goodie bag. Go." The young man runs out of the room.

Dirk turns to you and says grimly, "Change of plans. You are coming with me."

Michael Huemer

"An important point about anarcho-capitalism is that the transition to anarchy from the status quo matters. The transition favored by most anarcho-capitalists is not that we should start a violent revolution and just shoot everyone in the government. And it's also not that everyone in the government should just disappear overnight. Rather, the idea is that there should be a process in which the functions of the government are being shrunk while at the same time private institutions are expanding to take them over."

THE STATE

Dirk leads you out of the building and toward a short dock. Some men are already prepping a small, fast-looking boat. Dirk hops on, checks his radio, and starts powering the engine. You step down into the boat, and Dirk motions for you to sit next to him. A minute later, the young man from before runs up with a large duffle bag and drops it onto your lap. It is heavy and feels like someone has stuffed it with small packets. The young man hands Dirk a tablet and shouts that the other ship is sending a representative out on a dinghy. Dirk nods and engages the engine, and the two of you jet out toward the enemy.

"Tell me everything you know about your friend," he shouts over the engine.

You realize you do not know much about Big Billy. You describe his character and some of the things that happened on Danger Island. Dirk just grunts. When you get halfway to the enemy ship, Dirk turns down the engine to an idle and tells you to take the wheel.

"If there is any trouble, slam the throttle and steer us back to Freeport."

A few minutes later, a small boat approaches and pulls up next to you. It is carrying two men in uniforms. They are both armed. One of them throws a rope over to Dirk, who reels them in toward your boat.

223

Dirk has clearly done this many times, but you can see his thin frame struggle against the bobbing masses of the two ships. When the ships meet, the smaller of the two military men starts talking.

"I am a colonel of the Kenya Navy," he says.

"My name is Dirk, Chairman of Freeport."

"You will tell your military to stand down and prepare to be boarded."

"You want me to tell our military to stand down?"

"Yes."

"How can I do that?"

"What do you mean?"

"We do not have a military."

"I know you have guns in that place," he says, pointing to Freeport. "Well, we have three ships that could be here tomorrow, any one of which could sink your glorified barge. If you want to keep your shithole afloat, then you are going to submit and allow my men to board you for inspection. You are going to hand over records of all inhabitants and their biometric data. Once we are satisfied, then you are going to change course due West and anchor that trash heap off of our coast until further notice."

"You want to come aboard. Is your goal to hurt the people living here?"

"No."

"Then you and your men are welcome to visit. We do not want a fight. We only want to go peacefully on our way."

"I cannot let you go. We know you are involved in human trafficking. You will change course and anchor this vessel along the Kenyan coast."

"What makes you think we are involved in human trafficking?"

"This is not a debate. If you do not agree to our terms, you and your helmsman will be locked in our brig." You think he is talking about you, but he never looks your way.

"How can we come to terms if you have not heard our side of the story? Before things get out of hand, please take a look at this." Dirk holds up the tablet toward the colonel. "Watch our security footage and see for yourself."

The colonel makes no move. Dirk reaches across the divide to hand him the tablet, but the larger soldier growls and bats the tablet away. It slips out of Dirk's hand and lands on the edge of your boat. It teeters there for a moment, but Dirk awkwardly jumps on top of it to keep it from dropping into the ocean. Your little boat rocks from the shifting weight. A swell soaks Dirk's jacket, but he manages to protect the tablet. Tired, wet, and unsteady, Dirk plays a video on the tablet and holds it toward the colonel, but out of reach.

"You can see that my helmsman traveled to Freeport with the man you took aboard your ship. But how much do you know about your guest?" Dirk turns to you. "Tell the colonel what you told me."

You explain your trip with Big Billy and what you know about him. After about a minute, Dirk cuts you off.

"So you can see, this mysterious person came to Freeport of his own free will. He has been here for less than a week and spent most of his time stealing."

"I have no reason to believe you," the colonel says, but his tone is softer.

"We thought we were saving him, but he betrayed our trust, just like he betrayed your trust." Dirk plays another video and holds it for the others to watch.

The colonel stares at the video montage for a few minutes and then says, "Hawa mayi ya punda." You can see anger seeping into his face.

"As you can see, we did not kidnap anyone. You, on the other hand, may have already caught the real criminal. Pirate, thief, international drug smuggler—we are not sure who he is. But we think this bag might have been his." Dirk offers him the duffle bag, and the other soldier takes it. "You can keep it as evidence along with the tablet, as well as the stolen boat and radio. We will, of course, publicly thank you for scaring off the pirates that threatened us earlier this evening."

The other military man opens the bag to reveal a plethora of pills, powders, and other party favors. There are also digital storage devices. He looks up at the colonel hesitantly. The colonel takes a pinch of white powder and rubs it on his gums.

"There is no rush," Dirk says. "Freeport is slow, so you have time to decide what you would like to do. Better to be careful than quickly make a mistake. You are stronger and faster, so can come back whenever you like. You are in control."

"That's right." the colonel says. Then he thinks for a moment and shakes his head slowly. "We will review this evidence. You may maintain course for now," he says. He says something inaudible to the larger soldier, who pulls their rope back. A few moments later, their craft departs.

You watch them go for a moment, and then Dirk takes the wheel. He seems more relaxed and pilots the boat at a comfortable speed. As you head back to Freeport, you notice a few beholders positioned around the meeting point. Your boat is equipped with cameras and microphones as well. Dirk certainly likes to record things. Though you guess it was good that he had the footage of Big Billy.

You think about Big Billy and what will probably happen to him now that the sailors know the truth. You feel conflicted about it. He was difficult at times, but, without him, you might not have been able to excavate the *Margit*. Who knows how long it would have taken you to finish your boat then, if ever. You wonder if it was ethical to hand Big Billy over to the Kenya Navy and to give them fake evidence against him so they can prosecute him with unjust drug laws. You want to ask Dirk about it, but all you say is: "What happened to not paying tribute?"

"Oh, that? It was nothing. The contents of that bag were probably a year's salary for him, but drugs are cheap in Freeport. We are just lucky that we were dealing with someone seasoned and intelligent like the colonel. Every military has some individuals who want to protect liberty and are willing to use violence to do it. It is a good instinct. Every military also has a few soldiers who recognize that state militaries are just another government bureaucracy. Having only a thin veneer of righteousness, government militaries are slow and stupid, controlled by politicians for their own benefit, and not worth the hassle. An ordinary foot soldier would have mindlessly carried out orders, but the colonel has probably been around long enough to know better."

"We were saved by jadedness?"

"Self-interest, mainly. I also think he knew that I was telling the truth, and so he felt free to do the right thing. Had this been a top-down operation, I imagine the encounter would not have gone so smoothly. The world is lucky to have people who are willing to take bribes to do the right thing. Some governments have burdened their economies so much that they could not function without bribery."

"What would you have done if you weren't able to talk your way out of it?"

"Who knows? We could fight off pirates as a last resort, but fighting is not an option when it comes to most governments. Some of them are looking for any excuse to use their militaries. Those would jump on the slightest hint of violence as an excuse to kill or imprison us all. So violence is out of the question, but we have many plans in place depending on who and what we are dealing with.

"Fortunately, the decentralized nature of anarchy provides some protection against belligerent governments. People always have the option to disconnect from Freeport and go their own way. It may not be obvious, but this would be just as true on land as it is at sea. Imagine trying to take control of a territory where no central authority, no single point of failure, exists. It would slip through your fingers like baby jellyfish, stinging all the while."

"Is there anything you wouldn't do to protect this place? How can you be willing to hurt innocent people just to save Freeport?"

"Those military men might not know or understand what they are doing, but that does not make them innocent. They signed up to be part of an organization that exists to threaten and kill, not just undeserving foreigners, but even their own people. In a free market, soldiering would be a noble occupation. You could put your life on the line to fight evil and protect those who cannot protect themselves. On the other hand, national militaries mostly protect their government against its foreign and domestic enemies, often without regard to the lives of regular people."

"I was more thinking about Big Billy. Who knows what they will do to him?"

"I think I understand your question now. To be honest, Freeport is not the most important thing to me, and I do not think I would hurt an innocent person to protect it. Your friend was not exactly innocent, though. He would have brought down terrible violence upon us if he had convinced a military that we should be destroyed. Pirates know they are doing something evil, so they are practical about it. If the cost is greater than the reward, they will leave you alone. Governments have indoctrinated their militaries to think that they are doing something different—good and virtuous, even. So they are often willing to go to great lengths to achieve small victories. These kinds of soldiers will not hesitate to kill others, and they are sometimes ready to throw away their own lives as well. That mentality would make them heroic in a free society, but, under a state, it makes them especially dangerous.

"It is amazing how humans can be programmed. Something as terrible as war, so full of death and destruction, the cause of so much terror and misery throughout history, and still people can think of it as a duty, an honor. At least until they go through it themselves and see that they are not fighting for freedom, but for politicians. If they managed to get out without hurting anyone, then they are lucky. Others have to live with horror and guilt for the rest of their lives."

Dirk continues as he steers the boat up to the short dock from which you departed.

"War is just the path to a pointless, early grave. One day we will dig the biggest grave of all time and shove war in and cover it up. It is hard to do that now with governments indoctrinating children all around the world. You know, the way people are taught history out there, it breeds hate. This country invaded our country, so we hate them. It lasts for generations, even after all the guilty individuals are already dead. As if all the regular people tricked and forced the government into war, and not the other way around. The true pattern is that it is always governments against individuals. Either within their own territory or the territory of another government. You never see prime ministers dueling presidents, but always common people killing other commoners. Sure, there is small-time thievery, piracy, and murder across national borders, but all of that is insignificant compared to the destruction wrought by states. If we can get people to see that, then the world will start to change."

"Do you really think people will change their point of view just because some people are living large on a floating bazaar?"

"That worldview is the crux of it. Most of the people in the world do not see things the way we see things. To them, it is truly sad when someone in their community is murdered. They feel bad for the victim's family. But when they hear that thousands of people are dying from unintended consequences of some government's economic policy, they shrug it off as though it is not thousands of times worse. As if those people do not have families who love them and would give anything to get them back.

"And how many whip themselves into a joyful hysteria when their government kills masses of people in wars? As if those people did not have hopes and dreams. As if they did not deserve to grow up and fall in love. Government is a machine that consumes wealth and uses it to kill people. It is an engine of destruction. What is the difference between murder and war? They are the same thing, but government does it at a horrifying scale.

"Not every government makes war."

"True, but war is not the only way that governments kill. Many countries turn their aggression inwards, killing citizens for political reasons, disappearing dissidents, or committing genocide."

"Still, that's just some governments. Not all of them kill their own citizens."

"Not every country is as violent as another, but death by government is not always violent. How many have died because some bureaucracy did not approve a medical treatment? How many more died because their government restricts the number of people who can be doctors? Every time government interferes with the free market, someone has to pay the price. It may not be obvious, but occasionally people pay with their lives.

"Even those who survive are not safe. When people hear that a neighbor's home was invaded and some valuables were stolen, they are outraged. How could someone do that to another person? It is so violating to be burglarized. But tell them that taxation is extortion and they laugh. Haha, very funny. As if taxes were not theft of almost unimaginable magnitude. Billions of people being robbed every day. Every time they earn a little money. Every time they buy something, or sell something, or give a gift, or save for retirement. Everything they do makes them a target. Living itself becomes an excuse for being continually hounded by highwaymen. What is the difference between theft and taxation? They are the same thing, but the government does it at a horrifying scale.

"Not everything is taxed. Most countries don't tax food and clothing."

"Consider someone who only buys food and clothing. Say they are retired and have no income. They think they will just live out the rest of their days, safe, slowly drawing down on their savings. But savings are not safe. Do you know why counterfeiting is illegal?"

Dirk does not wait for a reply. "Creating fake money is not a crime in the libertarian sense. It does not hurt anyone. But when you spend it and pass it off as real money, it is fraudulent. Not only that, but you increase the supply of money in the economy. If all else is equal, prices for goods and services go up. You may have heard this called inflation. The counterfeiter gets to buy things for free, but then everyone else has to pay more for things. The counterfeiter is essentially stealing money from everyone else. It is an insidious type of aggression that slowly eats away the value of savings. And governments inflate the money supply as a matter of course, printing and spending new money every day. Not only that, but they market it as a service. As if inflation were helping the economy instead of hurting it.

"No individual counterfeiter could cause so much damage. People will naturally flee from money that is losing value. It is only when the government forces people to continue using the evaporating money that that big problems occur. That is another advantage Freeport has. People can use whatever money they want. In most other places, the national government monopolizes money production. Sometimes the government prints so much money that the value of its currency collapses to zero. Everyone laughs at those countries, but those are just the most obvious examples. More commonly, governments maintain a semi-stable rate of inflation, sucking wealth from everyone who uses their currency. This is a hidden tax that wreaks havoc on the economy. What is the difference between counterfeiting and inflation? They are the same thing, but the government does it at a horrifying scale."

You start to wonder if the whole world is Danger Island.

"When you look at history as one government causing enormous damage, and then another, and then another, you can see the real problem. Most of the people in any particular country are just normal human beings trying to live their lives, with no real desire to go to other places to rape and murder. There are a few, of course. Some join the military so they can kill with impunity. Some join the legislature so they can send brainwashed children to do the dirty work instead. But most are not like that.

"The Japanese soldiers who raped and murdered in Nanking deserve all our disgust, as do the American soldiers who dropped atomic bombs on the Japanese. But blaming all Japanese or all Americans is a huge mistake. Even more so if you try to blame the descendants of those who committed the crimes. There are very specific people in every country who deserve our ire, and the first place to look is the state apparatus. We should only hate aggression and condemn those who commit it."

A man and a woman help the two of you out of the boat and onto the dock. Dirk speaks to them briefly, and they run off. Then, the two of you begin walking back into town.

"What about supporting people who are fighting? How do you know whether the people you trade with are going to use your things for defense or offense?"

"We do not know, but if we were not in such a precarious position, I would trust business owners to figure it out. We have weapons for sale in Freeport, but no gun shop here is going to sell a firearm to someone who they think will use it to commit a crime. In the same way, no manufacturer is going to export arms to government militaries that will use them for war. Every weapon we might sell to a state would be used to subdue the people who live under it. People here could make a fortune, but they will not. It is the same principle.

"Not to mention that exporting weapons could be a PR problem, so most connection contracts prohibit it. The police contracts do not allow it, either. The same is true for exporting drugs to places where they are illegal and the like. Once the world catches up, we can lift these restrictions but, for now, it is too dangerous, and there are too many people watching us and waiting for an excuse to do us harm.

"It is sad because we really could help people who are suffering around the world if we traded with them. It is hard for people to worry about liberty when there are more pressing problems like food and clean water. The more people trade, the wealthier they will be. We can aid others not only with ideas, but also by helping them develop the means and motivation to push back against their rulers.

"It is not a perfect solution, but it beats the hell out of the political process. The great positive social changes in human history: the abolition of slavery, equal rights for women, etc., have not been handed down by benevolent rulers, but won as a result of working against, weakening, and delegitimizing governments. Maybe one day we will be able to catalyze peaceful revolutions around the world."

As you turn a corner, you see the building with the monitoring equipment. Dirk heads in that direction.

"I worry about the risks of getting involved in other people's problems, though. There are many people in the world, so many that I will never meet them all. I will never be able to save them all, but at least I can do my best not to hurt them. More than that—people have done so much for me, I wish I could help them all in some way. When I was first starting as an engineer, I felt so powerful. I could build anything and change the world. But then I read an essay called "I, Pencil" that changed my life. While reading that essay, I realized that true power comes from cooperation. People all over the world working together. People who do not know each other, and who will never meet, but see the price signals in the market and rush to each other's aid."

"I can build a machine, but only because someone else has made computer-aided design software. I can only use that software because someone else has created a computer. That computer only existed because a third person has built circuit boards. And on and on."

"It is a kind of friendship. All across the world, people working together. Cooperating with strangers and making the world a better place. Helping people they have never met and never will meet. I saw a video once of an interview with a cacao farmer. They gave him some chocolate. He liked it and asked where it came from. He had no idea people were buying his beans to make it. And there is no need for him to know. He specializes in his trade and others build upon it, inventing new products and increasing the demand for his services. We are all on one giant team."

You arrive at the building. The young man from before is waiting. He announces to Dirk that the Kenyan ship is still sailing along with Freeport but at a greater distance. Dirk eases himself into a chair. Then he slowly unknots his bow tie, leaving the ends hanging down his shirt. The young man hands him a drink.

"Sure, governments are always trying to stop us, but they are too slow and too stupid. All they can do is hamper progress and either try to take the credit when things go well or try to rationalize their existence when things go poorly."

"Can't the government just hire smarter people?" you ask.

"Of course, but it would not help. The people are not the problem, it is the sytem that is flawed. Economics shows why the incentives inherent in government will always lead to inefficient outcomes. Ethics shows that even apparent successes will be tainted by aggression."

"Is economics what inspired you to become an entrepreneur?" you ask.

"No. The purpose of economics is to logically analyze human action and choices. However, I like it as a tool to delegitimize the government and motivate libertarianism. It is unfortunate that most people do not understand economics. If they did, the world might be free next year. People would reject the state on purely utilitarian grounds. Many of the things it does are unethical and should not be done at all. Everything else can be done faster and cheaper by the free market. Governments have enormous opportunity costs in terms of income, wealth, and technology.

"But in the absence of government, it is not important for everyone to understand how the economy works. As long as people behave ethically, economics shows that people do not need to understand economics. Good things will happen naturally as people trade and cooperate in the free market. So, everyone can get along just fine without understanding any particular science, economics included. Just work and save money. And in a libertarian world, people would have the greatest incentives to behave ethically and get the benefits of cooperation for free, without knowing why. Hopefully, it will inspire many more to entrepreneurship, and many more will also be inspired to libertarianism. An environment of non-aggression would be the most significant catalyst for human progress. It maximizes the incentives for productivity and innovation, and, like nudging a satellite, improves the trajectory forever. This applies not just to the economy, but technology, culture, art, standards of living, and lifespan.

"Just two things stand in our way of all of these wonderful things: aggression and death. We know how to deal with aggression, but getting the world on board will be a lot of work. Governments exist because people support them. The same people we are trying to save are our biggest obstacle. We need to change the mental landscape, and that is going to take a long time. So long that I think the technical problem of mortality will be solved first, and worldwide libertarianism will come after. Probably neither will come in time for this old body, though." Dirk sighs. "So much to do, so little time."

You think about that while Dirk sends some text messages. A group of new people slowly gather in the room. Dirk tells you to go back to your hotel and get some rest. You would prefer to continue hanging around, but it is clear that you were only a part of the action by chance and nobody wants you around for the final act. You make your way back to your hotel room and lie awake for a long time before finally falling asleep.

Henry David Thoreau

"I heartily accept the motto, That government is best which governs least; and I should like to see it acted up to more rapidly and systematically. Carried out, it finally amounts to this, which also I believe—That government is best which governs not at all; and when men are prepared for it, that will be the kind of government which they will have."

DEATH & TAXES

You wake up on your last day at Freeport. You are finally going home. A whole day has passed since Big Billy's betrayal and the late-night confrontation with the Kenya Navy. You slept in yesterday and then spent the evening telling Annie the story. You were surprised by her reaction. She said that she always hated Big Billy, which is something you had assumed. The surprising part was that she said that, with time, she came to accept that it was useful to have him around. Even though he was the least hard-working of the three of you, and had no altruistic intentions whatsoever, the work he did do made life better for all of you on the island.

"Still," Annie admitted, "I wanted to leave him on the island once you finished the *Margit*. I never brought it up because I didn't think that I could convince you to do it, especially after he paid for passage. I thought it was a real risk bringing him with us. He could have attacked us, and there would have been nowhere to run. I'm such a sucker, though. Despite all the times he crossed the line, some part of me still hoped he would become a good person. Maybe even a friend. Well, now we know how that turned out."

How had it turned out? Big Billy managed to escape from Danger Island. Along the way, he never shared much about himself nor cultivated personal relationships with you and Annie. But over time he chose cooperation more and more often. Whether that was due to a change in heart or economic incentives, you may never know.

You had often wondered what kind of upbringing had produced someone who seemed, at times, to have total disregard for the lives of others. Now you wonder if there was something more you could have done to convince him to live peacefully with everyone else. It didn't seem like a knowledge problem that you could solve with better explanations about how the property system works or the benefits of cooperation. Big Billy was not stupid, he simply preferred to use aggression when he could get away with it.

It is not just eating habits, though. Big Billy has always preferred immediate gratification. Back on the island, he would do the minimum amount of work to survive and spend the rest of his time relaxing or causing trouble. If he ever chanced upon some surplus food, he would always binge on it rather than save it.

You realize that this personality trait means that Big Billy would have been stuck on the island forever. It took you a long time to save up enough materials to repair the *Margit*. You had to save a lot in order to have the time to do the repairs. It was necessary to produce more than you consumed. Economists call the difference between the way you and Big Billy behave "time preference." Big Billy prefers to enjoy the fruits of his labor sooner rather than later. Everyone does. However, the difference is that when given a choice between something now, and something better later, you are willing to wait for something better.

This process has fueled progress throughout human history. Savings lead to capital, which then increases productivity. The additional wealth allows people to spend time developing new technology, art, and other things that improve freedom. That opens up new opportunities for capital accumulation, and so on. But it all starts with saving.

Big Billy saw the savings of others as an opportunity to consume. In that regard, he was like many people around the world. Those who occasionally give in to aggression as a convenient way to get what they want. To steal a little when nobody is looking. To enforce their morality with legislation. To regulate away their competition. Or simply to get a little of someone else's wealth.

Aggression will always be a temptation. The best that can be done is to create incentives to choose cooperation. Annie was persuasive with her spear. Private security, social stigma, and lucrative job opportunities can be, as well. A society that disincentivizes conflict will help individuals minimize their own use of aggression. And each time a society makes large jumps toward this ideal, it becomes harder to go back.

You pointed this out last night, and Annie agreed. She gave the example of slavery. In the past, slavery was common. A few people spoke out against it but, in general, everyone went along with it because it was the normal way of things. The arguments against slavery back then were the same as now, perhaps even more visceral and compelling. Still, progress toward a more libertarian society took generations. Eventually the NAP won out, but the delay meant that millions of people had their lives ruined, not by plagues or famine, but by other people. And that, while usually no longer in the form of slavery, is still happening now. How long until the world removes the remaining institutions of aggression? Will it be generations? For the sake of the billions of people who suffer under them, you hope not.

The general mood last night wasn't all dark, though. Annie told you about an offer she got to play herself in a documentary about her unexplained disappearance and her sudden return. "I'll let you know who they cast to play your part," she said. It was kind of strange to think about someone else pretending to be you. You made a few suggestions and Annie laughed.

The two of you ended up staying up late, but, despite the sleep deprivation, the anticipation of leaving makes it hard to go back to sleep. You get out of bed and head to the bathroom. After a nice, long shower, you go to clean up and pack your things. Then you realize that you do not have many belongings to pack. Or even a bag to pack them in. You decide that you should buy a souvenir to bring home with you. You head out to shop and take one last walk around the city.

Freeport is beautiful in the nautical twilight. The muted morning colors and gentle sway make it seem that the city is under water. People are already going about their business, stores are starting to open, and it all seems so normal. But you feel something unusual that is hard to place.

As you walk through a park, you stop to appreciate the warmth of the sunrise. A new day. Another opportunity. When the sun becomes too bright, you turn away and see Dirk sitting on a bench nearby. You walk over to him.

"Hi, Dirk. I'm leaving today and wanted to say goodbye. Also, thank you," you say.

"Safe travels. When you get home, please let everyone know what it is like here," he replies.

"I will. It's strange; I have heard people say the only things guaranteed in life are death and taxes. I guess we'll have to take taxes off the list."

Dirk smiles at that for a long moment. Then he says, "Death and taxes—the two greatest enemies of mankind. I would like to say that we have defeated one of them, but the truth is that we have only pushed it back a little. Government still rules over most of the planet. All we have done is to show that life is better without it."

"Not better for everyone."

"Not in the short run, no. If I could press a button and make government disappear forever, then politicians would suddenly be unemployed. Bureaucrats would have to find productive work. People who were dependent on government would have to rely on friends, family, and charity. But in the long run, most people would be healthier, wealthier, and happier. It is hard to describe, let alone convince people of, the counter-factual. But without government, technology would improve at an unbelievable pace. It would save so many people from disease and hunger. Freedom would rise like the sun at dawn, and nothing would be out of our reach."

"That still leaves the other problem."

"Death? Death is just a technical problem, and eventually, technology will make it optional. That will be a nice bit of freedom. It is sad, but the fastest way to beat death is to rid the world of government. When we eventually solve the problem of mortality, I shudder to think of how many people we would have been able to save if not for government holding us back. Just more lives to add to government's unimaginable death toll."

"What do you mean?"

"People consider death and government to be very different evils, but government might as well be death's right-hand man. Forget all those who die because government holds back science and life-saving medicines. Governments have murdered so many innocents it is hard for the human mind to conceive. War, genocide, mass starvation. Millions of families snuffed out because some politician thought it would help him stay in power. Even if you discount the horrible wars that have happened throughout human history and only count people who have been killed by their own government, the death toll is still in the hundreds of millions. Humans do not have emotions that can reflect that level of devastation.

"Government is a parasite, so each one exists in a constant state of conflict with the people it dominates not to mention other governments. It leads to an unstable system. Given enough time, every government dies. The question is: When will we stop new ones from replacing the old? When will we stop repeating our mistakes?"

"Maybe never," you say.

"Maybe, maybe not. But those are the last great barriers to human freedom. I would say that they are the only problems that really matter. Once we only have nature to contend with, it is easy to see how things will go. Capitalism has already pulled people out of poverty and brought the world together. In the last few hundred years, extreme poverty has gone from affecting 94% of the world to single digits. There have been similar swings in literacy, access to food, child mortality, education, and many other areas of life. It is truly astounding what people can accomplish when they work together. What is more amazing is that private individuals have been able to work hard and achieve a much better world despite governments squandering their wealth and putting up barriers at every turn.

"Freedom has increased in most areas of life. Sure, there are occasional setbacks in specific places and horrible losses of life and capital every day. And yes, some people are working hard to enrich themselves while impoverishing society in general. But despite all this, modern society has rocketed forward with better technology, more education, more peaceful relations, and lifted billions out of poverty. Even a market economy hampered by criminals and criminal organizations is a truly awesome machine. In my small way, I want to be able to help drive progress around the world by participating."

"You've done more than most. Look at everyone here who is free thanks to you," you say.

"The free market has done such a good job that most people here, and even other people around the world, think they are free. But the truth is that we have a long way to go. Even in Freeport, we will not enjoy total liberty until the rest of humanity is living in a state of anarchy. Until then, we have to deal with the risk that some state might decide at any moment that we are a good target for their military. Or that we have offended their morals and need to be purified. Or some spy agency might take an interest in manipulating the management of our companies."

"Once humanity discards most of that insanity, we can focus on making life longer, more comfortable, and more fun for everyone."

"You really hate government," you say.

"Only because I see it for what it is. If someone gets robbed, they are furious about losing what amounts to a few percent of their income for the year. Government steals an order of magnitude more, then uses it to restrict their freedom. At least a thief leaves you alone after he has done his dirty work. The government stays with you, telling you what you can and cannot do, threatening you with jail if you do not listen, and taking a cut of every transaction you make. And what does it do with all that money and power? It uses it to indoctrinate the next generation of children so that no one will question the system they are raised in, no matter how unethical or immoral, no matter how much blood is on the hands of the state. It is just one continuous stream of crime interrupted only by periods of increased death and destruction."

"All I want is to put an end to the greatest criminal enterprises on the planet."

He takes a breath. His face is still stern, but some of the anger goes out of it.

"Alas, government is not some monster that I can kill with my hands. Even if every politician, bureaucrat, soldier, and spook disappeared overnight, people would rebuild their governments out of habit. The institution is a symptom of another problem—the real problem. It is an idea that every person must banish from their own mind. Without the support of the masses, government cannot survive. With their support, it cannot be destroyed. The people we are trying to save are the source of the evil we are trying to stop.

"I have done what I can, built an example for others to live by. I have even exorcised statism from a few friends with steady but gentle pressure. But I cannot convince the whole world on my own. We need every bit of help we can get. We need you. I will not ask you to lie or cast us in a false light. Just tell people honestly what you have seen. Freedom can work, and, when it does, the world will not be perfect, but it will be much, much closer to perfect. For the sake of those you love, and victims of government all around the world, help us. Do what you can. And one day, the survivors will enjoy something that seems impossible even to children who live in Freeport now: an everlasting world of peaceful cooperation."

You see tears in his eyes, but he does not speak further. He only nods at you as you turn to leave.

You feel a little shaken by the old man's words. Suddenly, you are not sure a souvenir is all that important. Maybe what you should take with you is not something physical, but something that represents the essence of the place. What you need to bring back are ideas.

You wander around aimlessly for a while. The sights and sounds that arise as the city continues to stir help you to relax. You stroll down some of the main shopping streets and look into the windows. Many of the stores are still closed, but you are not in a rush. You purchase some food and water for your upcoming trip and then start walking toward the dock where your ship will be waiting.

As you are getting closer to the dock, you hear Chelsea's voice from behind you.

"You weren't planning on leaving without saying goodbye, were you?" she asks.

You turn and see her walking up with a grin on her face.

She continues in a disappointed voice, "I thought that we were friends."

"I think that we could be friends," you blurt out honestly, and immediately feel a little embarrassed.

"Well, as my boss tells me, 'We are all friends in the free market,'" she says, finishing in a goofy voice.

When you don't respond, she asks if something is on your mind.

"If you had a choice between liberty and capital, what would you choose?"

"I think many people have that choice now. To get liberty, all you need is some remote spot where nobody will ever bother you. A little desert island somewhere in the middle of the ocean or a remote mountaintop. I imagine if you ask most people, even around here, they would say that 50 years under a typical government is better than 50 years alone."

"If you had to choose between liberty and death, what would you pick? Would you rather live free for 100 years or live under a state forever?"

"Oh, I think I'd move back home and live forever. Government is bad but, at least where I am from, it is bad at being bad. So most people can get along okay most of the time. Maybe that is the problem with government. It grows and becomes as big and evil as it can, but people keep it somewhat in check. So you end up with a system that is terrible but tolerable, so it never gets fixed.

"If you care about freedom though, I think you have to choose life. It's a prerequisite for freedom. When you're alive, you can do things. The more things you can do, the more freedom you have. If you die, you won't be able to do anything. Zero freedom. So you can think of death as the ultimate victory of nature over freedom.

"Government is horrible, but, as long as there is life, there is hope. We can teach people that there is a better way to live. Government is crime, and it's my job to put a stop to crime. In a sense, the state is every type of crime wrapped up and held together by fear and ignorance. We usually catch petty thieves, and a burglar eventually finds his way into the home of a gun owner. But government has reached a sort of semi-stable equilibrium. People hate it and what it does. They fight it. But others come to depend on it and support it. So humanity limps along, making progress, but only at a fraction of the pace that we could be going."

She pauses and says, "Why do you ask?"

You tell her about your conversation with Dirk.

"Oh, Dirk? Don't worry about him. He thought that once Freeport reached a certain size, it would start a trend—other free cities being founded or maybe even established cities seceding. Things are never that easy, so you can't let it get you down. If we worried about every initiative we started that failed, we wouldn't have entrepreneurs starting new companies or inventing new technologies. Why should it be any different for societal change? You keep trying things until something works. Honestly, I'm surprised that this giant raft even exists. So that is something, at least.

"Don't be like Dirk and worry about not being able to save the world. Just find the things you can do to help move us in the right direction, and do them."

Chelsea laughs. "Sometimes, I wonder if I am doing enough. All I do is keep people safe. But then I look around, and I think that there is a good chance that the kids growing up here end up immune to statism. They will see the world so clearly, understand it for what it is, and never be satisfied with the status quo. They'll build companies and technologies and shape the world in ways that we can't even imagine. I'm just a cop, but that's how I'll help. I'll protect them until they are ready, and that might be enough."

You smile, and then you and Chelsea say your goodbyes.

"Come back some time. I'll even give you a discount."

You tell her you will. As you walk down the dock, you think about her advice. What things could you do to chip away at such immense problems?

You could wait and watch while other people work out solutions. Many libertarians are focused on government and will continue to hack away at it. Sometimes they will make progress and sometimes there will be setbacks. Eventually, they may win and, if they do, it will be a stupendous milestone for freedom. But will you live long enough to see what happens?

You may get lucky. Government is a flawed, unstable system, so it is hard to predict what might cause it to collapse. It may expire sooner rather than later. You may even be able to contribute to the cause and hasten government's demise.

You may get lucky in another way as well. Government's expiration date is only one side of the equation. Technology is improving, and lifespans are increasing. You may not need to defeat government, but just bide your time until it disintegrates on its own.

Nothing is guaranteed in life. Neither freedom nor liberty. Neither death nor taxes. But while you are alive, you can still affect the world. Your choices can have an impact, both on yourself and on others.

You step inside the craft and sit down next to Annie.

"I got us some snacks," you say, handing her a bag. She takes a peek through it and then puts it down.

"I got you something, too," she says, and hands you a small felt bag.

You open it and take out a ring made of gold and an unusual black metal. The design is simple but striking. Every facet is there because the ring needs it—and for no other reason.

"I found a jeweler who makes them. She only sells them to those who physically come to Freeport, so I thought it would make a good souvenir. She said the black represents anarchy and the gold represents capitalism."

You thank her and put it on. You decide to let it be a reminder of the time the two of you spent together. It will also help you remember the valuable lessons you learned along the way.

Some of the things you learned are already starting to fade: Danger Island's geography, the currents around it, and how to build a hut. But some ideas are still firm in your mind: cooperation, conflict, and the effect each one has on the world.

You return to the possibility that, one day, governments will be replaced by peaceful institutions. It would be a great liberation. People would live longer, happier lives. Liberty would be more abundant than ever before.

But government isn't some technical problem that can be solved by a handful of freedom fighters. There is no single source of evil to destroy. There are only billions of people who passively or actively support institutions of aggression. Even if the government magically vanished, they would help the unscrupulous to rebuild it. The root of evil is not out in the world but in the minds of individuals.

Annie gently takes your hand. "We finally did it. We escaped."

You smile back and then turn to look out the window. You see men and women working on the docks and children playing in the street. Everything is peaceful and good.

But something is wrong. You managed to survive on Danger Island. You even managed to get away. You plugged back into society, where you can work and get whatever you need: food, clothing, shelter, and fun. You made new friends. Yet you still aren't safe. You, Annie, the people who live in Freeport, all the people around the world, are still in danger.

Danger Island isn't a place. It is a state of the world. It will exist everywhere and follow everyone until aggression and death are gone. For those who love freedom, it will be the greatest achievement of capital accumulation of all time, until the end of time. Without liberty, people can take away everything you have, everything you have built and sacrificed for. Without life, nature does the same. Until the world is rid of aggression and death, everyone is on Danger Island. The only way off is by working together. Cooperation is your most powerful tool, and libertarianism will allow you to wield it.

It doesn't make sense to worry about things you cannot change. But parts of the world can change. People can change. Every person who changes their mind about liberty will increase freedom in the world. Eventually, humanity will cast off old systems of oppression. Eventually, it will move beyond the limits of nature. Eventually, liberty and capital will be recognized as the map and compass of human progress.

There is a way forward. There is hope. Freedom is the answer. And now you understand it.

"Hey Annie," you say, "what was the message you put in that bottle?"

"Oh," she says, "I had forgotten about that."

You wait patiently.

After a while she says, "It was nothing, just a little poem," and then looks away.

You wait, pointedly. She tries to ignore you, but eventually relents and recites it from memory:

> "Our friendship weathered
> Danger Island's summer storms
> and sailed for freedom."

EPILOGUE

Annie seizes the script, her hand flashing forward and a pencil ripping across its pages, slashing raw black lines over the sentences. Her hand goes on razing words, commenting, rebuilding in furious strokes. The script reads like an economic treatise. Annie puts it down and calls her agent.

"The story has potential," she says, "but the dialogue is awful. Tell them to read it out loud until it sounds like how humans talk. Can we afford to bring on a second writer?"

Her agent says that he will look into it. Annie goes on.

"I got the headshots. This second one won't work, and it's my fault. I'm sure my description of his personality threw you off. He was actually quite handsome. And bigger. Yes, really."

Annie pauses to listen to a stream of complaints about money. She turned down a lucrative contract to work on this pet project, and that upset more than a few people. *Well, it's my life, and I am going to do what I want.*

"Another thing," Annie cuts in, "We can do all of the beach and ocean shots locally, but we'll need to go to Freeport for some of the filming."

As expected, she hears a wave of objections. Then she smiles and says, "Who is going to stop me?"

...

Chelsea wonders aloud how she managed to get herself into this. She calmly accounts for her situation: surrounded, outnumbered, and outgunned. She has never been in a firefight before. That is the beauty of living in a city where everyone is free to carry firearms—nobody wants to pick a fight. I guess it had to happen eventually, she thinks.

She looks around. One has taken cover behind a fence, and two are in the shadows of a nearby building. Another is up in a lemon tree. It looks hopeless.

Except for one thing. Last night, she had received an anonymous tip. A concerned parent had warned her about the gang that she is now facing, warned her about the weapons they had collected. She had heeded that warning and came prepared. Not enough to save herself, but at least enough to take some of them down with her.

Chelsea resigns herself to her fate and reaches into her bag. Her hand wraps around the grip, and she takes one last look around. One of her adversaries shouts, "She has a weapon!" and they open fire.

Chelsea drops the bag and lifts out the largest water gun she could buy. Within two heartbeats, she returns fire. Her firearms training and superior range even out the playing field. She instinctively dashes about and takes a few hits, but manages to blast the one by the fence right in the head. The one hiding in the lemon tree only ends up getting himself wet as his stream bounces off of leaves and branches. The two that stuck together scream and make one final charge. They soak her from behind, but she strikes back with precise jets to their chests and chins. That sends them squealing and running home. The one by the fence races after them. The one in the tree just sits there, crying. Chelsea helps him down.

"Now, now, don't cry. Trying is how you learn."

The child runs off, sniffling. Chelsea assesses the damage. Her shirt and hair are wet, but, otherwise, she is unharmed.

Chelsea packs up her water gun and makes a record of the event in her log. She smiles at the thought of her manager reading it. Probably won't get a promotion for this one.

...

Dirk looks over the estimates again to make sure they are right. Then he calls one of Freeport's largest investors.

"I have just sent over the numbers. Please, take a look."

There is a long pause. Then Dirk hears the reaction he was expecting: disbelief.

"How long has this been going on?" the investor asks.

"It was made public yesterday, but my contacts tell me that the company was founded two years ago. They have been operating in stealth mode since then."

"Who is financing their operation?"

"All private investors, just like us."

"How do we stop them?"

"We cannot," Dirk says.

"There must be something we can do. They are copying us. Why didn't you patent some of these ideas?"

"And then what? Beg some government to shut them down?"

Dirk looks at his watch. Another meeting coming up soon.

"Your philosophy won't matter if we all go bankrupt. We'll have to scrap the whole project."

"We will just have to innovate. Find ways to make Freeport more attractive."

"It is more than that. They have a new business model. Fewer sections, faster cores, and more services."

Dirk leans back in his chair and folds his arms. "That is a good idea," he says.

"Don't compliment them, think of a solution. Ten of the sections aren't renewing their contracts. We are starting to lose."

Slowly, a smile spreads across Dirk's face.

"No, we are finally starting to win."

Glossary

Freedom is the ability to do what you want.

Capital is anything that people value.

Human action is purposeful behavior.

Praxeology is the study of purposeful behavior.

Cooperation is when people interact and their actions are compatible.

Conflict is when people interact but their actions are not compatible.

Liberty is the absence of conflict.

Aggression is any action that causes conflict.

A **free-market** is a society without conflict.

Ethics prescribes how to resolve conflict.

Morality defines whether an action is good or bad.

The **non-aggression principle** is an ethical rule against causing conflict.

Libertarianism is an ethical system that resolves conflict with the non-aggression principle.

Property is any scarce means of ethical human action.

Ownership is using a scarce resource in an ethical way.

The **private property system** is a tool for following the non-aggression principle.

Justice is undoing the consequences of aggression.

A **social norm** is a convention for action.

Capitalism is a libertarian social system that assigns ownership according to the private property system.

Anarcho-capitalism is pure capitalism.

Government is any organization that society exempts from the non-aggression principle.

Anarchy is the absence of government.

Further Reading

For a New Liberty by Murray Rothbard

Machinery of Freedom by David D. Friedman

The Problem of Political Authority by Michael Huemer

Human Action by Ludwig von Mises

The Economics and Ethics of Private Property by Hans-Hermann Hoppe

Chaos Theory by Robert Murphy

The Ultimate Resource 2 by Julian L. Simon

Defending the Undefendable by Walter Block

Bourbon for Breakfast by Jeffrey Tucker

Against Intellectual Property by Stephan Kinsella

Economic Laws of Scientific Research by Terence Kealey

How I Found Freedom in an Unfree World by Harry Browne

Economics in One Lesson by Henry Hazlitt

Libertarian Quandries by Jakub Wisniewski

Acknowledgements

I would like to thank Michael Malice for his mentorship throughout the writing and publishing process.

Thanks to Simon Franek for helping to improve all aspects of the book, especially the ethical theory.

Beta-readers: Anders Mikkelsen, Yuriy Skobov, Dominik Franek

Editing: Hugh Barker, Susan Cahill, Harry Painter, Barry Lyons

Portrait Artwork: Milos Ckonjovic

Cover Design: John Girgus

Cover Photo: "I'll go my way" by Damian Gadal, edited from original (bit.ly/2J3y1wZ), licensed under https://creativecommons.org/licenses/by/2.0/

About the Author

Kris grew up in New Jersey and then studied engineering at Carnegie Mellon University and the University of Pennsylvania. He has a background in robotics, artificial intelligence, and software engineering. He is a professional entrepreneur who has built several technology companies.

For more information, please visit krisborer.com

Made in the USA
Coppell, TX
30 July 2020